MEDIEVAL
& RENAISSANCE
INTERIORS

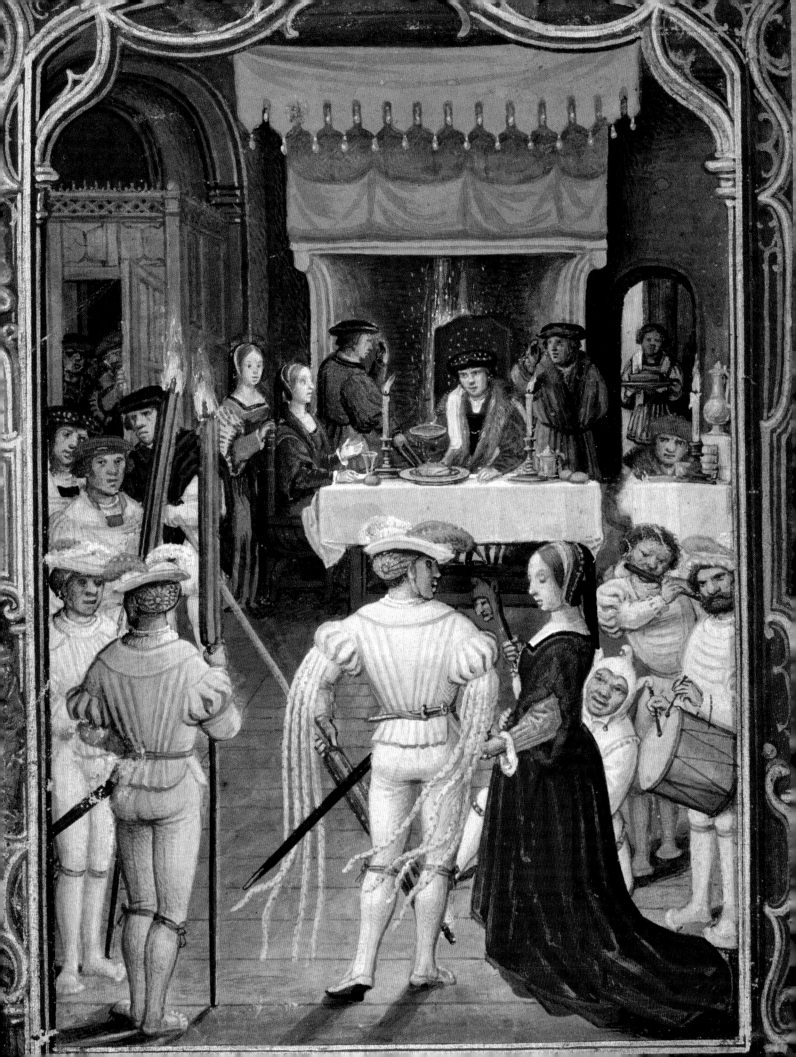

MEDIEVAL & RENAISSANCE INTERIORS

in Illuminated Manuscripts

EVA OLEDZKA

First published in 2016 by
The British Library
96 Euston Road
London NW1 2DB

Text copyright © Eva Oledzka 2016

Illustrations copyright © The British Library Board and other named copyright-holders 2016

ISBN 978 0 7123 4973 4

British Library Cataloguing in Publication Data

A catalogue record for this publication is available from the British Library

Designed by Briony Hartley, Goldust Design
Printed in Hong Kong by Great Wall Printing Co.

Page 1 see [84]
A brass candleholder on a Gothic table. The table is covered with a tablecloth and stands next to a buffet. The vista indicates that this room is likely to be in a castle. The walls are faced in stone or painted in imitation, and the floor is paved with stone slabs.

Miniatures attributed to the Master of the *Chronique scandaleuse,* Pierre Sala, *Petit Livre d'Amour*, France, Paris and S. E. (Lyon), first quarter of the 16th century; British Library, Stowe MS 955, fol. 8

Page 2 see [70]
Calendar page for February. Feasting and dancing in a hall. The opulent fireplace dominates the interior.

Simon Bening and workshop, Book of Hours (Golf Book), Bruges, probably early 1540s; British Library, Add. MS 24098, fol. 19 v

Page 6 see [43]
The translator Simon de Hesdin at work. This study is bare and looks rather uncomfortable but is nevertheless charming. It is furnished with a lectern and a long bench running along the walls. The window is partially glazed, with multi-coloured glass in its upper part. A wooden lattice in the lower section provides privacy. The shutters consist of several parts, which can be opened or closed independently. The cupboards are quite interesting: two are in the wall niches and have doors decorated with Flemish linenfold panelling. Another cupboard, or a simple open shelving unit, is fixed to the wall. The undecorated plastered walls seem to be scratched and neglected. The inscription reads 'Je suis bien/Toudis Joieulx/1479'.

Master of the White Inscriptions, Valerius Maximus, *Facta et dicta memorabilia* (translated by Simon de Hesdin and Nicholas de Gonesse), Bruges, 1479; British Library, Royal MS 18 E III, fol. 24

CONTENTS

a briefte et
fragilite de
ceste dolereuse
vie linconstan
ce et variable
te de fortune
la mutacion aussi de la voulente
et de la pensee humaine sont les
causes pourquoy ie nay point
fait a ce commencement le pro

logue de ce liure. Car ie peusse
bien auoir prouine ou auoir eu
en voulente de celle chose faire
qui moult tost et legierement
peust auoir este empeschee par
aucune des causes deuant dict.
toutesuoies par maniere dun
petit preambule Il me fault faire
aucunes declaracions neccessai
res pour lentendement de ce liure

I

INTRODUCTION

Illuminated manuscripts often give us a unique glimpse into medieval and later life in castles, palaces and houses in urban and rural settings, but they are an underused resource. Countless images in manuscripts, unknown to many and rarely published, depict houses and households. Illuminations frequently reveal long-lost details of a very wide range of architectural elements, furniture, luxury goods and even objects of everyday use. Often we can discern not only the forms and decoration of private surroundings but also the materials used. Some of the illuminations contain astonishingly minute detail and crispness in their representations, and their quality is occasionally comparable to that of famous panel paintings and murals depicting similar subjects. Most of the existing research on illuminated manuscripts concentrates on traditional art-historical aspects. This book attempts to show how illuminations reflect domestic interiors and provide information on them, conveying the broad context not only of cultural trends but also of private life and customs in medieval and Renaissance Europe.

The majority of the illuminations chosen for this publication come from the British Library's own manuscript collections. These are supplemented by several additional visual resources and miniatures from other libraries and museums. The best depictions showing interiors date from the fifteenth to the mid-sixteenth century and were produced in France, Flanders, Italy, England, Germany and Poland. The discussion of the subject therefore concentrates on the social and stylistic aspects of Gothic and Renaissance domestic settings in these countries and focuses on the cultural supremacy of Flanders and Italy, the European trendsetters of the time. Romanesque miniatures showing interiors, which are very stylised and, although beautiful, rendered far less realistically, are also briefly considered and illustrated with a few examples.

One has to bear in mind that the Italian interiors and their representations discussed here, usually fifteenth-century, fall into the stylistic Renaissance bracket, while contemporary counterparts created elsewhere are referred to as Gothic and medieval. The Renaissance cultural movement, with its humanistic ideas and artistic style, developed at a time when interest in Antiquity was being revived and indeed rapidly becoming all-encompassing, and it had its beginnings in Italy in general and in Florence in particular. The Renaissance spread and flourished in Italian city states long before it was gradually introduced north of the Alps, where it was accepted in modified versions and eventually became established. The process of cultural transition was very gradual and fluid, but it was in the sixteenth century that Europe's main transformation occurred. The year 1500, admittedly an extremely artificial milestone, is generally considered to be a universal, pan-European boundary between the Middle Ages and the Renaissance.

In contrast to publications that present research on architecture and art objects associated with and commissioned by the ruling political and intellectual elites, this book attempts to consider medieval and Renaissance European interiors at all levels of society. Although representations of interiors inhabited by the ruling classes prevail in existing pictorial sources and in this publication, they are supplemented by images of households of merchants, craftsmen and peasants. The wealth of illuminated material showing daily private life in castles, palaces, country residences, townhouses and cottages allows us to explore some of the similarities and differences in the home settings and depicted lifestyles of all classes.

This book focuses on domestic interiors and looks at various parts of the house. The persistent lack of diversification in room functions and the difficulty in interpreting images of them is taken into account in the structure of this publication. Rather than discussing houses room by room as we know them now, it concentrates primarily on the elements of the domestic architectural shell, and its furniture, fixtures and fittings. Some aspects of multifunctional interiors, used for private and work-related activities or official functions, are also explored. Essential pieces of furniture such as beds, chests, tables, benches and chairs were predominant in medieval and Renaissance houses. Textile wall hangings were a desirable addition, to complement the ambience while adding insulation and decoration. Specialisation of room functions, although visible in numerous Italian designs and documented in inventories and contemporary descriptions of royal, princely or aristocratic homes, was still an unfinished process in most non-elite north European houses. This is reflected in representations of interiors and in documents. Detective work is often needed to establish whether a described or depicted room is a hall, a bedroom, a kitchen or a study, and it can be inconclusive, as many rooms were multipurpose. It is nevertheless important, wherever the attempt is possible, to discuss pieces of furniture in their primary context in the house layout. It is likely that a bed would normally be represented in a bedroom and a desk in a study, so bedrooms and studies are examined together with their primary pieces of furniture. In the case of the study, this also encompasses key items and implements specific to that environment. Halls are not discussed in detail, as these were the epitome of multifunctionality. Instead, we shall look at the material culture related to them (tables, buffets, luxury tableware) and the role they played in the phenomenon of status display, which took place mainly in halls. This is especially relevant in the context of the exceptionally informative masterpieces of fifteenth-century illumination chosen to illustrate the topic. Finally, although some widely depicted luxury articles are discussed, low-status objects such as pottery, glass and pewter have had to be largely omitted owing to the multitude of regional variations and the lack of any very detailed representations in miniatures.

In order, crucially, to consider this subject in a wide cultural context, some institutional interiors and exteriors, both secular and ecclesiastical, are also taken into account. We shall also frequently refer to other types of selected contemporary images (easel paintings, murals, woodcuts), written sources, material evidence, such as surviving buildings and their decoration, and museum pieces.

This book is intended as a general introduction to the topic, though a few interesting examples of focused scholarly research have been included. Unfortunately, a full and homogenous treatment of the topic is not yet (and may never be) possible, as any survey depends on the type and nature of the relevant research carried out to date. The subject of domestic interiors, their associated material culture and the visual resources depicting them is vast and interdisciplinary, encompassing mainly history, art history and archaeology. The nature of the relevant research is varied and detailed but – more importantly here – fragmentary, isolated and usually concentrated in narrow aspects of selected scholarly disciplines. A further problem is the disjunction not only between historical vocabulary and modern terminology but also between the kind of data used in studies in the neighbouring disciplines of art and history, which are frequently not standardised and often not directly compatible and comparable with one another. The resulting information, although fascinating, is not easily analysed and extracted or transferable into a single publication, let alone synthesised into a uniform general introduction. Consequently, this publication does not attempt to serve as a scholarly study or a handbook and, being neither, should not be consulted by those in search of comprehensive data. It also does not consider in full detail the complex issues of the realism of representations. A scholarly discussion of relevant research aspects has been undertaken by the author in her doctoral thesis, which is an interdisciplinary examination of the subject. The present text and the illustrations accompanying it are put together to allow a glimpse of medieval and Renaissance domestic interiors in a broad and general cultural and historical context, aiming principally to provide the reader with an enjoyable visual resource supplemented by background information. It hopes to inspire those less familiar with the topic to study it further and not only to consult other specialist publications on related subjects but also to explore it themselves in archives, libraries, museums, galleries and historical places.

e ventre matris mee vocauit me dñs
nomine meo. et posuit os meū sicut
gladium acutum sub tegumento

II

The Context of Domestic Architecture and Interiors

1. Representations of Domestic Interiors in Art

INTERIORS IN ILLUMINATIONS

Medieval and Renaissance illuminated manuscripts are books written by scribes and illustrated by painters on vellum, parchment or sometimes paper. Up to the twelfth century most manuscripts were produced in monastic scriptoria and were destined for church use. Illuminated books of this period mainly contained religious and biblical Latin texts, very often the four gospels of Matthew, Mark, Luke and John, or the Psalms. After the foundation of the first universities in Paris, Bologna and Oxford, secular production centres started to emerge there and in other cities across Europe, supplying books for church, education and private use. Town scriptoria continued to produce devotional books, often with commentaries, but added to their repertoire popular lay prayer books (called books of hours) and literary or historical texts, such as the Arthurian romances and works by classical authors. Gradually, Latin started to give way to vernacular languages. Illuminated books were mostly commissioned, though some were also made for the open market and purchased by both ecclesiastical and secular patrons. Many luxurious manuscripts decorated with masterpieces of miniature painting were destined for royal collections. Illuminated manuscript production continued after the introduction of movable type in the 1450s. Miniatures were added to a few high-end printed books but traditional manuscript illumination flourished continuously and went from strength to strength up to about the mid-sixteenth century, especially in Flanders, France and Italy. They are found to some extent throughout Europe, but it was also initially in Flemish, French and Italian art that the most realistic representations of domestic interiors and their associated material culture and architectural context appeared and developed (Fig. 1, 49, 53, 83, 125, 126). It is therefore no coincidence that the vast majority of illuminations in this publication were produced in the fifteenth and sixteenth centuries in those countries. They outnumber the English, German and Polish miniatures of domestic interiors, and this reflects the varying frequency of illustrations and the different levels of popularity of such illuminations across Europe.

[1]
The Birth of St John the Baptist. The scene is set in an affluent late medieval northern European interior. A large bedstead is surrounded by opulent red textile hangings held up by ropes fixed to a wooden beamed ceiling. The chest is open and its contents are visible, including a small compartment for valuables. A buffet, which has doors decorated with Gothic tracery and a lock, stands in the middle of the room. It is probably used to store precious objects as well as the metal, glass and ceramic tableware standing on top and on the shelf under it. Other pieces of highly polished brass tableware and candleholders are kept on a shelf fixed high above the doorway. The spinning wheel, here kept in the bedroom next to the buffet, was used on daily basis by diligent women. The window is fully glazed and along the wall under it is a bench covered with comfortable cushions. The doorway allows a view of other rooms arranged in an enfilade. Above another door, at the back of the house, hangs a devotional image.

Attributed to Jan van Eyck (Hand G), The Turin-Milan Hours (*Les Très Belles Heures de Notre Dame* of Jean de France, Duc de Berry), Flemish, 1422–1424; Museo Civico, Turin, 467/M, fol. 93 v

[2]

[2]
Dunstan as a bishop, writing his commentary of the Rule of St Benedict. Early miniatures are heavily stylised, two-dimensional and focus on foreground scenes presented against an abstract geometric pattern or a gold gilt backdrop. Later illuminations depict three-dimensional, realistic-looking interiors.

Smaragdus of St Mihiel, *Expositio in Regulam S. Benedicti*, Canterbury, Christ Church, *c.* 1170–*c.* 1180; British Library, Royal MS 10 A. XIII, fol. 2 v

[3]
St Jerome in his cell. St Jerome is seated on a bench at his desk and writing in an open book. His cell is filled with study equipment and ascetic symbols. The room has a vaulted ceiling, bare stone walls and a floor paved with green glazed tiles. The lower openings of the window are fitted with round glass pieces, while the top openings have grilles. The window surround is splayed and profiled and its head is arched. The arch adds stability to the window and the splaying lets in additional light. Next to the window are a simple writing desk and a curving bench. A hanging above the bench and a bolster provide some comfort. Several books are placed on the window-sill and one on the bench. More books and other objects are kept in the side compartments of the desk. The desk is fitted with a large crucifix and a tape holding scissors, writing implements and bits of paper or parchment. On the shelf above St Jerome's head stand numerous glass bottles and a brass candleholder. Below it are suspended an hourglass, an astrolabe, a rosary and brushes. The lion at St Jerome's feet is his traditional attribute. The miniature is based on a famous woodcut executed in 1511 by Albrecht Dürer, though the window has been added by the illuminator. Dürer's images of St Jerome in his cell or study were in turn probably inspired by Italian art.

Stanislas Claratumbensis (Samostrzelnik), Prayer Book of Sigismund I, King of Poland, Kraków, *c.* 1524; British Library, Add. MS 15281, fol. 1 v

Early, mainly Romanesque miniatures illustrating the subject were typically very stylised and focused on monumental figures equipped with some accessories but presented against largely abstract, ornamental backdrops. Only marginally and loosely classifiable as showing domestic interiors, they are illustrated here with just a few examples (Fig. 2, 17, 82, 132).

Illuminations showing scribes at work can demonstrate the above generalisation (Fig. 2, 132). Frequent since the sixth century, early and high medieval depictions focus on the scribe himself and strongly idealise his surroundings, which at the time of monastic book production were more likely to be ecclesiastical and institutional than secular and private. Further, they also demonstrate a problem of anachronisms. Most such miniatures represent saints or the four evangelists and come from religious manuscripts. Popularised in many countries by the migration of illuminators or of the books themselves, they repeatedly replicate to various geographical locations templates transmitted over several centuries. This obscure and complex process makes many early illuminations unreliable as a tool in the study of the chronological and regional variation of interiors and their associated material culture. Late medieval and Renaissance illuminations, although not entirely unproblematic, are more dependable. Fourteenth-, fifteenth- and sixteenth-century miniatures, while still often making use of shared designs, gradually show more realistic, contemporary domestic settings and recognisably local architectural elements, including furniture and fittings characteristically diverse in form and decoration. Produced in secular workshops – those of city or court artists – and often illustrating books of hours used for private devotion, many late medieval and Renaissance miniatures abandon earlier iconic portraits of idealised saints or evangelist-scribes and replace them with images of author-scribes shown in their well-appointed, regionally distinct and apparently domestic studies. However, with the growing dissemination of prints, some late fifteenth- and sixteenth-century miniatures once again become increasingly based on pan-European templates: woodcuts. Luckily, these are relatively easily identifiable (Fig. 3).

Like depictions of scribes, many other illuminations showing medieval and

Renaissance domestic settings come from religious manuscripts and illustrate Christian subjects. Among these, portraits of the four Evangelists, Annunciations and Nativities were the most popular (Fig. 1, 11, 63, 98, 107). Calendar pages for January, February and sometimes December included in books of hours are the most predictable place to find secular images of interiors: most of them show people sitting at a table in front of a blazing fire (Fig. 4, 12, 53, 70, 125, 126). Literature (mainly medieval romances), chronicles and other history books also include numerous illustrations of house interiors (Fig. 8, 43, 76).

One has to bear in mind that even if many illuminations show rooms identifiable as halls, studies, bedrooms or even kitchens, more often the function of the interiors illustrated seems to be unclear. Even in the case of images apparently depicting a specific type of strictly specialised room it is difficult to be certain, as miniatures show only a portion of it and one can never be sure how the rest of the associated interior was equipped and used. In numerous miniatures even the most recognisable and seemingly specific rooms, such as bedrooms and studies, are frequently depicted as multipurpose interiors (Fig. 5, 6, 7, 72, 104). While some illuminations may be based on templates that predate them by several decades, and could therefore show a traditional way of living, new compositions are likely to record a contemporary status quo and therefore probably reflect a slow specialisation of domestic space in most non-elite houses.

Diversification of room functions first developed in medieval royal and aristocratic private quarters in castles and palaces. For instance, English castles and manors had specialised rooms by the fourteenth to fifteenth centuries. Diversification of the house layout seems to have become less elitist and reached heights of sophistication in Italian Renaissance houses, both for the middle classes and for patricians; at a later stage, generally in the sixteenth century, it gradually became fashionable across Europe in lower-status, middle-class households. As cultural developments and fashions usually percolate down from the top of local society, the slow diversification of room types in northern Europe may be due to the makeshift nature of many upper-class households. To at least some extent, this can be illustrated by examples from the Bedford Hours miniatures showing interiors inhabited in the early fifteenth century by the Duke and Duchess of Bedford (Fig. 9, 45, 56). Assuming that at least some of the interiors shown there are domestic and not ecclesiastical, these miniatures demonstrate how textile hangings could create private living spaces within larger interiors (see pp. 61–3, 79).

Although many houses had multiple rooms, these were often used for various purposes. Strict specialisation of room functions as we know them now seems to have been slow to develop in northern Europe. Although traceable in inventories and other documents relating to the homes of the nobility, it is not easy to find in illuminations or in other visual sources. As mentioned, the specialisation of domestic space throughout society was considerably developed in Renaissance Italy. As in royal houses, it also reflected the need for social display but, as room specialisation was of patrician (usually banking and mercantile) origin, it was not based on house ordinances, nor was it linked

[4]
Calendar page for January. A man is warming himself and feasting by a fire, which is burning on an open hearth. Some meat is curing in the smoke. The man is sitting on a decorative seat and drinking from a *hanap*; he is heating up the contents of a large pot. On a trestle table behind him are a metal wine jug, a chalice, a serving bowl with meat, a bread roll and a knife. Here the room doubles as kitchen and dining room. Many medieval houses had just one multifunctional room like this, which at night would be turned into a bedchamber. The trestle table could be dismantled to make room for bedding. Specialised rooms developed very gradually and even affluent Renaissance households would still have multifunctional rooms.

Psalter, Liège, third quarter of the 13th century; Bodleian Library, University of Oxford, MS Add. A. 46 , fol. 1

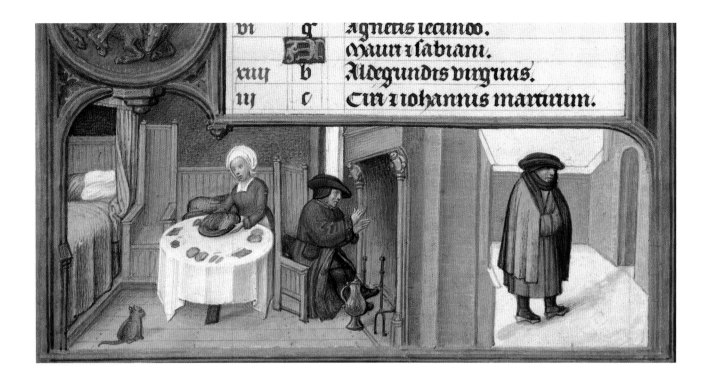

agnetis tecunco.
Maur ı fabıanı.
xııı b Aldegundıs vırgınıs.
ıı c Cırı ı ıohannıs martırıum.

[5]
Calendar page for January. The scene is set in a well-appointed walled townhouse or country mansion. A comfortable multipurpose private chamber like this, called a parlour in England, would include a bed and sometimes a fireplace, and could be used for meals. The room is fitted with a matching joined and linenfold carved suite consisting of a bedstead, two high-back chairs, a bench and a wall panel, possibly detached from the wall. The presence of such a panel makes this illumination quite rare as these are not easily identifiable in manuscripts. This may be due to the size and to the composition of illuminations, since panelled walls are frequently and clearly depicted in larger contemporary Flemish paintings. The grey stone wall, visible above the timber elements, is bare and undecorated, as are the wooden floorboards. The bedstead is adorned with a functional but also very opulent headboard and hangings, throws and cushions. The fireplace has carved corbels and elegant iron firedogs. The man is warming a large pewter wine jug at the fire and the woman is setting the table with a dish with meat, bread, trenchers and cutlery. The scene is patiently supervised by a cat. Pets are frequent features in miniatures and cats were often shown in action hunting mice.

Attributed to the workshop of the Master of James IV of Scotland, Book of Hours (Hours of Joanna I of Castile), probably Ghent, *c*. 1500; British Library, Add. MS 35313, fol. 1 v

to the noble ritual. Instead, it arose from the need for comfort and from appreciation of the beauty and sophistication of Renaissance design, appealing to all classes and eventually becoming widely popular beyond Italy also. The trend was introduced and rapidly developed by fifteenth- and sixteenth-century Italian urban elites, who preferred a settled life and favoured classically inspired architecture and interior decoration, so it was in Italy that this tendency was first documented in contemporary written and pictorial evidence. The best northern examples of images of rooms adapted to settled urban life come from Bruges and Ghent illuminations showing built-in and decorated *en-suite* furniture ensembles. However, these can also make it very clear that, as late as in the sixteenth century, well-appointed affluent rooms were still used in a multitude of ways. Characteristically for northern Europe, they are conservatively Gothic in style even though they were produced around 1500. Both points are exemplified by the January calendar scenes from books of hours produced *c*. 1500 (Fig. 5, 6). The miniatures show rooms furnished with large beds and sizeable dinner tables. Both furniture pieces are equally important as features defining the use of the room, which in consequence seems to be a combined bedroom and hall or dining room. Such rooms were probably multipurpose private chambers. In England they were called parlours.

In spite of the sophisticated theory of Renaissance architecture, there are also contemporary depictions of multipurpose rooms in Italy, though they are well appointed and Renaissance in style. A January calendar scene from the Hours of Laudomia de' Medici attributed to the Florentine illuminator Giovanni Boccardi, for example, is an almost perfect match for its counterpart in the above-mentioned Bruges and Ghent illuminations. In all likelihood, the Italian illumination reflects the discrepancy between the proposed ideal of Renaissance elite living and the traditional, informal, more down-to-earth but still affluent daily practice in the cradle of the Renaissance itself, Florence, and in the surrounding countryside (Fig. 7).

[11]
Annunciation scene set in a Flemish bedchamber. The Virgin is kneeling at a wooden *prie-dieu* covered with a green fabric, and is reading a book. A decorative maiolica vase with two handles and cobalt decoration is standing behind the Virgin on the tiled floor. In the background we see a typical Flemish bedstead with a carved headboard. The bedcovers and hangings are of opulent red fabric. Next to the bed there is a suite consisting of a high-back box chair and a bench. The bench is a piece of furniture with a dual purpose, serving both as a bench with a backrest and as a chest for storage of valuables. Such chests had a hinged seat and could be fitted with a lock. On the chair and on the bench lie comfortable, warm cushions, which were often made of good wool or velvet. Next to the bench stands a a buffet. It matches in style the other pieces of furniture, and its doors, like the rest of the woodwork in the room, are decorated with typically Flemish late fifteenth-century linenfold carving. Such cupboards are normally depicted as being used to store vessels, ewers and other objects. An interesting detail can be seen above the buffet: a curtain. Judging from the position of the curtain, it covers a religious painting. We can assume this on the basis of pictorial evidence and descriptions found in inventories. There are other Flemish illuminations showing uncovered religious paintings placed above buffets, and inventories often state that some paintings were placed behind their own curtains. Note that many book illuminators also worked as panel painters and that this illumination, like many others executed in the same milieu, shares its composition with earlier and contemporary Flemish panel paintings.

Master of the David Scenes in the Grimani Breviary, Book of Hours, Flanders, beginning 16th century; Bodleian Library, University of Oxford, MS Douce 256, fol. 48 v

PATRONAGE AND CULTURAL LINKS

Although some peasant and artisan interiors are present in medieval and Renaissance art, these are infrequent and most of them seem sanitised, romanticised and fragmentary (Fig. 12, 53, 68, 72). Depictions of the best French interiors come from illuminations showing royal and ducal settings, while fifteenth-century Flemish and Italian art often portrays an aspirational middle-class context (though elements of upper-class interiors are sometimes also depicted).

The motives for commissioning art and architecture in general and representations of opulent middle-class domestic settings in particular seem to be similar in Flanders and Italy. Rooted in comparable phenomena, such as thriving banking, trade in luxury goods and (especially textile) industry, this type of patronage led to numerous developments in the domestic material culture and decorative art. In Italy, possibly to a greater extent than in Flanders, patronage became a powerful political weapon for upwardly mobile patricians.

When one thinks about iconic and realistic-looking images of medieval interiors, Flemish early fifteenth-century panel paintings probably come to mind first. The particularly striking Annunciation scenes by the Master of Flémalle and Rogier van der Weyden showing the Virgin Mary in her room, mentioned above, were influential for at least a century. These panel paintings belong to the first known northern European images placing Annunciation scenes in domestic interiors. The rooms are very luxuriously appointed. They have the best possible architectural fittings: opulent fireplaces with sculpted corbels, glazed windows (with stained glass inserts, lattices and shutters), tiled floors and, in the Mérode Altarpiece, a *lavabo* niche. Van der Weyden's Louvre *Annunciation* has a beautiful and luxurious bedstead. Although sparse, the furniture looks very comfortable and possibly expensive, especially the benches with convertible backrests and buffets. These ensembles are supplemented by very valuable and typically Flemish domestic fixtures: the *lavabo* is fitted with a brass laver and a linen towel suspended from a decorative rack, there are brass candlesticks on the tables, and further decorative candleholders are attached to the chimneypieces. The Virgin Mary is shown reading books – luxury articles in their own right. Valuable (and appreciated mainly for the skill required in their production) maiolica vases and lavish fabrics complement the interiors. Although the patrons of these paintings are often not known, such interiors are very likely to show rooms in wealthy merchants' houses. Most fifteenth-century Flemish painters worked in very prosperous mercantile centres such as Brussels, Bruges and Ghent, and their clients often came from merchant and banking families who, in emulation of the Burgundian nobility, strived to display their wealth, sophistication and piety. Commissioning a painting depicting the Virgin Mary in a bourgeois house was an ideal and a very ingenious way to achieve all of these objectives and additionally to buy one's way out of purgatory. The Virgin is shown inhabiting patrician rooms, surrounded by luxury fixtures and fittings: 'trophies' and indicators of material success accumulated by a merchant or a banker. Earthly goods bought by sometimes unchristian means – of which usury was considered by the church to be one of the worst – are revalidated and reassessed in these images. Through association with the Virgin Mary, the room and its contents are assigned a Christian meaning and elevated to the status of religious symbols, consequently putting their patron's mind at rest.

The composition and some of the details of van der Weyden's panel paintings showing Annunciation scenes were replicated in countless miniatures and became typical for many late fifteenth- and early sixteenth-century Flemish illuminations produced in Bruges and Ghent, as designs and patterns were shared in and between workshops, passed on from masters to pupils and remained popular with patrons (Fig. 11, 63).

This type of imagery was equally popular in Italy, where there was a similar rationale behind commissioning art. As many of the surviving images of Italian interiors predate

[12]
Calendar page for January. The interior and exterior of a cottage.

Simon Bening and workshop, Book of Hours (Golf Book), Bruges, probably early 1540s; British Library, Add. MS 24098, fol. 18 v

[13]
A couple in their bedroom. This miniature appears to copy the composition of Jan van Eyck's panel painting the Arnolfini Portrait, dated 1434 and now in the National Gallery, London.

Attributed to Maître François, *Valerius Maximus*, translated by Simon de Hesdin and Nicholas de Gonesse, *Les Fais et les Dis des Romains et de autres gens*, Paris, between 1473 and *c.* 1480; British Library, Harley MS 4375, fol. 70

the fifteenth-century Flemish masterpieces, it is possible that the fashion for depiction of middle-class interiors was to some extent introduced to Flanders by Italian patrons. The argument is supported by the fact that many Italian merchants and bankers had branches of their businesses abroad and their principal and most affluent outpost was Bruges, an important port and art centre in late medieval Flanders. Some Italians are known to have commissioned panel paintings from Flemish artists. Jan van Eyck's Arnolfini Portrait is the best example of a Bruges bedroom inhabited by Italian patrons. Echoes of this painting are also found in later illuminations (Fig. 13).

The astronomical wealth of Italian fifteenth-century bankers and merchants – accumulated at astounding speed – combined with their extraordinary political aspirations and the spread of Renaissance humanistic thought to fuel patronage and thus to accelerate the development of a flourishing art market, predominantly that of Florence and the rest of Tuscany. This in turn resulted in revolutionary changes in art and in ecclesiastical, secular, civic and domestic architecture and interior design, which had to match the ambitions of their patrons. Middle- and upper-class Tuscan – above all Florentine – late medieval and Renaissance houses were especially sophisticated. The architectural design and interior decoration of these buildings publicly flaunted and celebrated the importance and power of the leading families and their political aspirations.

The Medici and numerous other Italian banking families spent vast sums on patronage

to develop Renaissance thought, and on all types of visual high and decorative art. Their financial means enabled them to put a stamp not only on the interiors but also on the exteriors of their houses, on the communal space in cities and on the landscape of the countryside. Their patronage of private and civic architecture, still surviving for everybody to see, also found its way into illuminations commemorating their sophistication and power. One of the Florentine miniatures from the Hours of Laudomia de' Medici, executed *c.* 1502 by Attavante degli Attavanti, does just that: it shows an iconic and clearly recognisable image of the Palazzo Medici, not only the first 'purely' Renaissance residence but also the seat of the principal patrons of Renaissance art (Fig. 14).

From about 1500 and long before European rulers co-opted the ambitious Medici into their dynasties, they accepted the classical, Italian Renaissance ideas, adding them to their own very strong Gothic traditions. But northern European cultural trends and innovations also influenced Italy. This was particularly true of Flemish fifteenth-century material culture and art. For instance, Bruges not only matched the financial and artistic climate of Italy but, as one of the seats of

[14]
Visitation scene. In the background, the Palazzo Medici, Florence. Commissioned by Cosimo de' Medici and designed probably by Michelozzo in 1440s, this building provided a template for many other Renaissance houses. The masonry of the façade is divided into three horizontal zones. The entrance leads to a central, symmetrical courtyard and from there to a garden at the back of the building. Ground floors of Italian houses in mercantile cities such as Florence and Venice were typically utilised for practical purposes, mainly business. The courtyards were also used for large banquets or wedding receptions. The first floor (*piano nobile*) was a principal living space and housed the main hall (*sala*). According to inventories, next to the *sala* in the Palazzo Medici was the bedroom of the head of the family, his study and a family chapel. It is only in the chapel that the original fresco scheme, Benozzo Gozzoli's *Procession of the Magi*, has survived. The Medici study was as famous as the chapel and housed numerous spectacular treasures. The large windows of the *palazzo* are biforate. Their openings have round arches and are divided by colonettes. The space between the tops of the colonettes and the round arches encircling each set of two openings is decorated with roundels. The illumination records the palace's appearance before the two corner entrances were turned into windows in 1517. The palace is embellished with Medici insignia (*palle*), as is San Lorenzo, the Medici family church, which can be seen at the back of the square. The depicted façade of the church is fictive and could be based on one of several contemporary designs.

Attributed to Attavante degli Attavanti, Book of Hours (The Hours of Laudomia de' Medici), Florence, *c.* 1502; British Library, Yates Thompson MS 30, fol. 20 v

the Burgundian dukes and their court, considerably surpassed the Florentine mercantile elite in its political status and connections with European royalty. As the elevated political standing of the Burgundians was relatively new and shaky in the fifteenth century, the forces driving the Italian Renaissance art markets, especially the need for magnificent display of power and wealth, were equally visible in the mercantile and upper classes in Flemish culture, and strongly influenced the sphere of domestic design. Other states recognised the cultural supremacy and remarkable achievements of Burgundy and Italy, adopted numerous elements of their culture and incorporated them into mainstream European society and its architectural and artistic makeup.

2. Painters and Manuscript Illuminators as Interior Decorators

Painters and manuscript illuminators are now considered artists. In the Middle Ages, however, they were usually classed as craftsmen and performed a variety of jobs. Medieval books on the craft and art of painting, such as Theophilus Presbyter's *De diversis artibus* (written in the early twelfth century) and Cennino Cennini's *Il libro dell'arte* (written *c.* 1400), and some from the Renaissance, mainly stressed learned skills, knowledge of techniques and ability to handle materials, rather than creativity and talent. Medieval and Renaissance court painters, among them also manuscript illuminators, are documented as having performed a variety of decorating and other mundane duties in elite households. Others who had their own workshops also often influenced the look of interiors in a multitude of ways and produced many kinds of decorative art. Most of the artistic output across Europe, including that for domestic use, was devotional in character, and panels and statues of the Virgin Mary, of Christ and of the Saints were produced *en masse* during this period. However, other types of household objects in various media, and wall decorations – sometimes abstract – were also executed by painters.

Jean Bondol, an illuminator ranked a *valet de chambre* at the court of King Charles V of France, provided cartoons (design drawings) for the cycle of the Angers Apocalypse tapestries, woven by Nicholas de Bataille for the king's brother Louis I, Duke of Anjou in the 1370s in Paris. Bondol's cartoons are known to have been based on illuminations of an Apocalypse manuscript. The surviving tapestries belonging to this cycle fill a whole sizeable room and are a very vivid example of luxurious wall decoration in fourteenth-century royal French interiors.

Manuscript illuminations must have served as a basis for decoration schemes on numerous other occasions as well. For example, a manuscript of *Faits des Romains* was used as a template for the life of Julius Caesar painted by Jehan Coste for the Dauphin of France in 1350s at the castle of Vaudreuil. It is also possible that a 1256 contract between King Henry III of England and Master William the painter refers to a commission to decorate the king's wash-room using a design based on a manuscript illumination. The picture was to show a king being rescued from plotters by his dogs. Such images are known from contemporary thirteenth-century English bestiaries.

Skill in the handling of various materials, supplemented by creativity, was also crucial for the fourteenth-century French and Burgundian court post of *maître des engins et des peintures*, a combined job as master of paintings and of artifice/mechanical inventions. At the residence of the counts of Artois, the Château de Hesdin, this post was inherited within a painter family and held by Jacques, Laurent and Hugh de Boulogne. The definition of artifice and mechanical inventions seems vague but we know that Melchior Broederlam, a Fleming from Ypres employed by the dukes of Burgundy as *valet de chambre* who also worked as a *maître des engins*, served as a painter and a designer of textiles and of

[15]
King David. King David sits on an x-framed chair with lion-head finials. A floating cloth of honour, probably silk, is attached to the rod above his head. The stylised background of the illumination imitates geometric patterns used for medieval painted wall decoration.

Master of the Bible of Jean de Sy, Guyart des Moulins, *La Bible historiale complétée* (Genesis–Psalms), Paris?, 1357; British Library, Royal MS 17 E VII, fol. 231

tiled floors. It is probably no coincidence that the Annunciation scene of his 1390s altarpiece of the Charterhouse at Champmol, Dijon, shows exceptionally beautiful tiled pavements. Decorative pavements were considered an attractive feature of both ecclesiastical and domestic interiors and often feature not only in paintings but also in illuminated manuscripts. It is also possible that the intricate, colourful geometric background patterns of numerous manuscript illuminations, especially from the fourteenth century, could have been based on, or otherwise closely related to, contemporary floor and wall decoration (Fig. 15, 16, 54, 57, 101, 102, 108).

Later, Renaissance court artists also took on roles akin to *maître des engins et des peintures*. In the 1490s, for example, Leonardo da Vinci held such a post at the Milanese court of Duke Ludovico Sforza. The jobs Leonardo carried out in Milan ranged from portrait and religious paintings (such as the *Lady with an Ermine*, now in

[16]
St Luke in a study, seated under a cloth of honour at a revolving lectern. There is an open bookcase at the back of the room. The bottom half of the wall is panelled, the rest of the wall surface above the panelling is decorated with a medieval multi-colour geometric pattern.

The Dunois Master (associate of the Bedford Master), Book of Hours (The Dunois Hours), Paris, *c.* 1440–*c.* 1450 (after 1436); British Library, Yates Thompson MS 3, fol. 15 v

the Czartoryski Foundation at Kraków in Poland, the *Last Supper* in the refectory of the Convent of Santa Maria delle Grazie in Milan, and the two *Madonna of the Rocks* altarpiece paintings, one now in the Louvre in Paris and the other in the National Gallery in London) to interior decoration (such as the ceiling and top portions of walls painted with *trompe l'oeil* trees in the Sala delle Asse in Castello Sforzesco, Milan) and designs for stage sets, costumes and installations for festivities held on the occasions of Sforza family weddings (such as *La Festa del Paradiso*, staged in 1490 in honour of Isabella of Aragon, the young wife of Gian Galeazzo Maria Sforza). Leonardo is considered an iconic, perfect example of a rounded Renaissance man and a talented artist: accomplished as both an inventor of genius and a brilliant painter, he was able not only to use the traditional knowledge he learned in his master's workshop, and copy and represent reality, but also to go further and to design and create new machines, miraculous for his time, and, in his pictures, a divine and supernatural world of perfect beauty. Leonardo, arguably to a greater extent than other gifted Renaissance artists, fulfilled traditional medieval beliefs in the painter's proximity to the sacred, divine power of devotional images of Christ (such as the so-called *Veronica* representing Christ's face), of the Virgin Mary and of the saints, and met Theophilus' and Cennini's expectations of the learned skills of painters. Yet he also fulfilled the expectations of L. B. Alberti and of other fifteenth-century Italian humanists, who believed that painting was not a mechanical activity but an intellectual one, and as such a noble, liberal art.

Many other Italian painters, especially those working in fifteenth-century Florence, combined craft and art successfully. Their traditional, learned technical skills were paired with astonishing creativity fuelled by humanist thought and the developing Renaissance. Numerous paintings and other art objects produced at this time in Florence and in the rest of Tuscany were destined for homes. Giorgio Vasari in his sixteenth-century *Vite* gives many examples of celebrated fifteenth-century painters who decorated furniture, such as chests or wall panels. One of them, Sandro Botticelli, executed such work for Florentine elite circles. His painting *Venus and Mars* (now in the National Gallery in London) is known to have been part of the furnishings, possibly in a Vespucci household. Its original function is still unclear: it used to be considered to have been a *cassone spalliera* (a panel associated with a chest) but, according to recent research, it was possibly associated with a bed or a bench. Another Botticelli picture, *Primavera* (now in the Uffizi), was listed in a Medici inventory of 1498 in the bedroom of the Florentine townhouse of Lorenzo di Pierfrancesco de' Medici. It formed an ensemble with a *lettuccio* (a daybed), above which it was suspended. Botticelli and his workshop also executed historiated domestic wall panelling and frescoes. In 1480s his workshop painted four panels (*spalliere*) with the story of Nastagio degli Onesti for a bedroom of the Palazzo Pucci, and frescoes of *Venus*, the *Three Graces* and the *Seven Liberal Arts* in the Tornabuoni family's Villa Lemmi in Florence (these are now detached and in the Louvre in Paris).

Other Florentine fifteenth-century painters, among them illuminators, also contributed to interior decoration and furniture production. For instance, the illuminator Apollonio di Giovanni owned a workshop producing painted chests, which were usually commissioned on the occasion of a marriage. Many elements of the chests were prepared by others but Apollonio painted (at least some of) the historiated panels. The style and subjects of his known illuminations (such as the 1460s *Aeneid* of Virgil, Biblioteca Riccardiana, Florence, MS. 492) and of his chest panels are very similar. Tuscan chests usually do not survive in their original form, as many of them were dismantled over the ages and/or unsympathetically restored. Their attractive panels were often isolated from the pieces of furniture to which they belonged and 'recyled' as paintings. Two such panels from Apollonio di Giovanni's chests are now also separated from chests they decorated and are displayed as detached paintings on the walls of museums (in the Ashmolean Museum, Oxford, and the Museo Correr, Venice).

3. Architectural Elements in Illuminations

Architecture has always been present in illuminations, initially as abstracted constituents, and later as ideal or real sweeping townscapes, or detailed views of the exteriors and interiors of castles, palaces and churches. Architectural borders and frames constitute a major group within this category of manuscript decoration. Many Byzantine mosaics,

Gothic and Renaissance murals, and especially religious panel paintings or carved altarpieces in ornamental frames (often commissioned and created for specific spaces and therefore fitting in with them aesthetically) copied architecture directly from church or palace interiors or façades, and illuminations did the same. This is especially apparent in countless high medieval miniatures that show prominent figures and clearly mimic wall niches, canopied tabernacles or *aediculae* (shrines framed by columns) containing statues. The first depictions of architectural elements, mainly columns and arches, as ornaments in illuminations come from the earliest of known miniatures. The tradition not only survived but indeed flourished right through to the end of illuminated manuscript production, and then lived on in print (Fig. 13, 17, 18, 35, 58, 97, 100, 103, 105, 107, 131, 134, 139).

Painted decoration representing architecture usually mirrored the artistic style rooted in the intellectual ideas predominant within the illuminator's cultural milieu and lifetime, although anachronisms are also known, usually when an artist copied older illuminations or workshop patterns.

Architectural settings could encase text and image alike. If combined with an illustration, they sometimes fused with it and became an integral part of the image. This is especially noticeable in numerous miniatures portraying secular or ecclesiastical figures of authority, such as rulers and saints, usually either free-standing or, respectively, occupying a seat of honour or sitting at a lectern. The earliest of these images are stylised, many as otherworldly as Byzantine church mosaics, and stress the elevated position of their subjects by means of decorative schemes often consisting of columns, pediments or arches, combined with luxurious fabric draperies and dazzling abstract, frequently gilded

[17]
Nativity scene. The Romanesque architectural setting frames and provides a backdrop to the main narrative.

Gospel Lectionary, Germany, Swabia (possibly Hirsau), first quarter of the 12th century; British Library, Egerton MS 809, fol. 1 v

[18]
St Matthew in his study, sitting on a seat of honour with an attached writing or reading board. The miniature of the evangelist is surrounded by an elaborate Gothic architectural border and illusionistic curtains. In Flemish houses such curtains would have been drawn to cover domestic devotional paintings or sculptures when they were not being used for prayer or contemplation (see also Fig. 10 and 11).

Master of the David Scenes in the Grimani Breviary, Book of Hours, Flanders, beginning 16th century; Bodleian Library, University of Oxford, MS Douce 112, fol. 25

backgrounds. Early miniatures of evangelists found in religious manuscripts constitute a very large group of such images and are predecessors of fifteenth- and sixteenth-century illuminations showing them, other authors, scholars or even artists, placed in a realistic Gothic or Renaissance interior, either a study or a workshop. Portraits of scholars (scribes, translators or authors) executed in this manner can often be seen on frontispiece illuminations. The majority of miniatures showing evangelists at work precede their writings, and provide pictorial headings; many of those showing authors in realistically rendered domestic interiors originate from books of hours, which became enormously popular in the late Middle Ages. Most of these were produced in fifteenth- and sixteenth-century Italy, France and Flanders, especially in Bruges workshops (Fig. 18, 134).

Late medieval and Renaissance presentation scenes, also occupying an honorary position at the beginning of manuscripts and showing authors or translators and their patrons, seem to be descendants and amalgams of ruler and scholar representations. They usually depict the scholar at work when visited by his patron in his study or, more frequently, the scholar handing over the bound manuscript at the patron's quarters in a ceremony often witnessed by courtiers (Fig. 8, 46, 62, 82).

In many fifteenth- and sixteenth-century illuminations, it seems to have been just as important to render interior and exterior architecture realistically, in order to provide an illusionistic backdrop, as it was to portray the actual narrative and protagonists. The lifelike scenes can be embedded within an additional, yet separate, architectural border, which often resembles a more or less elaborate picture frame. However, a group of Flemish illuminators of books of hours produced in the second half of the fifteenth century and the first half of the sixteenth century took such frames to another level of artistry and created a vast array of very intricately designed architectural borders that were both naturalistic and yet clearly imaginary (they were truncated, and did not obey the laws of gravity), mimicking ecclesiastical and secular exteriors and interiors (Fig. 18).

4. Domestic Exteriors and Interiors in Town and Country

Because of the scope of this publication, it will only be possible to give the briefest overview of domestic architecture. However, any discussion of representations of European medieval and Renaissance domestic interiors has to be interpreted in the wider context of their setting, especially that of architecture, which was very diverse in form, internal structure, style and building materials. Depending on their form and function, most houses of the period are usually referred to as castles, palaces, townhouses, manors or cottages, but the typology is by no means clear-cut (Fig. 12, 14, 19, 20, 21, 22, 24, 25, 68, 89).

The function of a house not only determined its external appearance, it also influenced its internal layout, which in time evolved considerably and became more and more sophisticated. Deeply rooted in political, cultural and social causes, this process was also a clear expression of an essential and increasing need for privacy and comfort. Thus, gradual changes in the layout of house interiors eventually resulted in the development of individual rooms and their specialisation as we know them, or refer to them now: sitting rooms, dining rooms, bedrooms, studies, kitchens, bathrooms (Fig. 1, 3–7, 11, 13, 16, 72, 80, 81, 107, 114, 125, 126, 137). Other major advancements in domestic architecture of that period occurred in the heating and lighting of buildings. Glazed windows, fireplaces and tiled stoves became the norm in houses, and provided not only basic secure shelter but also reliably protected the inhabitants from the elements and offered comfortable and healthy living conditions (Fig. 8, 10, 13, 43, 50, 67, 77).

Stone, brick and timber are commonly considered to be the building materials used in high-, middle- and lower-status architecture respectively. Although this association holds true in many cases, the choice of fabrics usually depended on the regional differences in availability of natural resources. Accordingly, stone was more frequently used in southern Europe, while north of the Alps timber and brick houses were more typical. Wealthy patrons could sometimes afford fashionable imports but they often chose to adhere to local traditions. On the other hand, trends were important. Accordingly, in the second half of the fifteenth century, at the time of Burgundian cultural supremacy, Flemish brick courts such as the one in Ghent and Bruges were enthusiastically copied in England, a country rich in good stone. Obviously, many building materials were often mixed to varying degrees in one building (Fig. 19, 20, 21). In Venice, for example, many buildings would have timber foundations supporting brick walls and elaborate stone façades, as in the exquisite Ca'd'Oro built for the Contarini family in the first half of the fifteenth century.

[19]
The Crucifixion with a view of Paris. Realistic surroundings showing contemporary European landscapes, cityscapes, house interiors and other regional details were often included in devotional images. This made the scenes more immediate and brought them closer to the viewers. The houses appear to be built mainly of stone and brick.

Charles, Duke of Orléans; Pseudo-Heloise, Poems; *Art d'amour; Les demands d'amour; Le liver dot grace entire sure le fait du government d'un prince*, London and Bruges, last decade of the 15th century; British Library, Royal MS 16 F II, fol. 89

[20]
A view of London. The old London Bridge with buildings on it is in the background, and in the foreground is the Tower of London. Duke Charles is shown in his rooms in the White Tower. The houses are built of stone, brick (?) and timber.

Dutch artist working in London?, Charles, Duke of Orléans; Pseudo-Heloise, Poems; *Art d'amour; Les demands d'amour; Le liver dot grace entire sure le fait du government d'un prince*, London and Bruges, last decade of the 15th century; British Library, Royal MS 16 F II, fol. 73

[21]
A Polish city view (detail from a crucifixion). This cityscape, possibly of Kraków, then Poland's capital and the location of the main seat of the king, shows Gothic and Renaissance townhouses typical of late fifteenth- and early sixteenth-century southern Poland. Although timber buildings were still quite common in villages and smaller towns of the region, which was extremely rich in timber, many houses in Kraków were of brick and stone. In a rich and densely built-up city this was not only for display or ceremonial reasons, but also for security and fire safety.

Pontifikal Erazma Ciolka, Kraków, early 16th century; Princes Czartoryski Foundation, Kraków, RKPS 1212, fol. 194 v (detail)

Castles are popularly considered to be archetypes of medieval architecture. These high-status fortified residences dominated the areas surrounding them and were built in the best possible strategic positions, frequently on cleared hilltops and overlooking vast stretches of land, roads and rivers. Inhabited by royalty and the nobility, medieval castles had defensive origins and, while the provision of lodgings and administration were important, the security of residents was the original and prevailing purpose. Therefore, in spite of encompassing private lodgings for the lord's family, their courtiers and servants, large kitchen complexes, chapels and other auxiliary buildings, the key attributes of castles were of military origin and included moats, curtain walls, bastions, battlements, arrow-slits, gatehouses, drawbridges, portcullises, turrets, towers and keeps. Although the first medieval castles were often timber structures, later ones were built mainly of stone or brick, which allowed construction of larger edifices and offered increased protection (Fig. 22).

Palaces, typically in both the Middle Ages and the Renaissance, were luxurious royal, aristocratic or patrician residences where the principal function was ceremony or display. Not able to withstand a siege in the same way as castles, palaces were frequently built within cities (Fig. 23). However, as castles were the epitome of the architecture of chivalric power, many of the castle's characteristics found their way into palaces, townhouses and manors, thus sometimes making the distinctions between building types unclear, especially in the residences of the nobility.

A large proportion of townhouses belonged to the middle- or working-class population and served as both family lodgings and places of business. Artisans' workshops, bankers' premises and merchants' warehouses and shops could all be accommodated at home. This was both secure and convenient, as often all family members lived and worked together. Townhouses were regionally very diverse and, depending on the wealth of their inhabitants, could range from humble sheds to Venetian or Florentine palaces. The poorest among the population would live and work in one rented room. Servants or apprentices often lived and worked with their masters and shared their premises. The majority of prosperous artisans or merchants would probably devote one part of a house to lodgings and another to work. Reception rooms – Italian s*ala* or German g*ute Stube* – were customarily situated on the first floor. The same floor, the *piano nobile* of Italian Renaissance houses, could accommodate bedrooms, studies and even chapels. The kitchen in an Italian townhouse would often occupy the top floor, while in a northern European household it would frequently be banished to an outbuilding. Lower floors, as less private spaces, were favoured for work. Shops were habitually on the ground floor and even very affluent Florentine or Venetian merchants would utilise the ground floor of their family palace for business. However, in northern Europe – for instance in the southern German city of Regensburg – merchants preferred to trade in impressive vaulted cellars. Space in attics could also be used for the storage of goods.

A townhouse built north of the Alps would usually have a narrow façade, consist of several floors, have annexes at the back of the house, and could have gardens in the mews. These cramped conditions were a necessity typical of old city centres where plots were divided into narrow, long strips to provide room for new buildings with direct access to main streets and squares (Fig. 24). A southern European townhouse, on the other hand (except in Venice, where the often very narrow façade faced the canal), tended to stretch along the street and have a broader façade. Haphazard urban sprawl was remedied by town planning, which developed considerably in the Renaissance. It culminated in the foundation of new towns such as Pienza (Italy) or Zamość (Poland), which were designed in line with humanistic ideals.

Although towns tended to have some agricultural space within the walled area, as this enabled the population to survive a siege, many prosperous burghers would draw some of their food supply from their farms or country estates, which sometimes also doubled as country retreats. As investing in land was both prudent and prestigious, inhabitants of cities often owned farms, some of which were turned into splendid villas, manors or fortified residences (Fig. 25).

The most basic type of medieval and Renaissance village dwelling was a cottage or a farmhouse. Most of these were inhabited by free peasants or serfs, were constructed from the cheapest available material (timber or stone depending on the region), and had a very simple layout. Generally, early farmhouses initially consisted of one multipurpose room with a central hearth used for both heating and cooking. From the later Middle Ages hearths were gradually replaced by fireplaces. Separate kitchens or bedrooms were extremely rare in buildings of this type. Animals and crops were often kept under the same roof but usually in separate parts of the house (Fig. 12). Farmhouses, just like grander

[22]
Calendar page for March. A Flemish moated castle (or a fortified manor) with a drawbridge.

Simon Bening and workshop, Book of Hours (Golf Book), Bruges, probably early 1540s; British Library, Add. MS 24098, fol. 20 v

[23]
Calendar page for May. A Flemish city wall and gate.

Simon Bening and workshop, Book of Hours (Golf Book), Bruges, probably early 1540s; British Library, Add. MS 24098, fol. 22 v

[24]
Calendar page for June. Jousting competition in a Flemish town square.

Simon Bening and workshop, Book of Hours (Golf Book), Bruges, probably early 1540s; British Library, Add. MS 24098, fol. 23 v

[25]
Virgil's Georgics. An Italian village.

Attributed to Bartolomeo Sanvito; Virgil, Pseudo-Ovid (*Georgica* (ff. 17–58), with argumenta), Rome, between 1483 and 1485; British Library, King's MS 24, fol. 17

[26]
Medieval Bakery. Baking ovens, being a potential fire risk, were often located in separate buildings. In larger country houses or mansions they belonged to a set of outbuildings used for food preparation. In towns they were commercial ventures baking and selling bread and pastries. In Italy, for example in medieval Florence, bakers also roasted pre-prepared meat dishes brought to them by clients, who then collected them the same day. See also Fig. 27 and 78.

Psalter, Ghent, *c.* 1320–30; Bodleian Library, University of Oxford, MS Douce 5, fol. 8

manors, could also be surrounded by simple outbuildings, and kitchen gardens would also be contained within the enclosure. Other, more distant outbuildings and village spaces could be communal and shared with neighbours. Some agricultural buildings, such as barns and granaries, were very impressive. These well-designed and beautiful structures usually belonged to manors and provided safety and security for crops, which was absolutely essential for survival. Some of these gigantic medieval timber barns and Renaissance stone granaries still survive in England and Poland respectively.

Grander country residences, such as English manors or Italian villas, came in many shapes and sizes. Occupied predominantly by the ruling classes – patricians, gentry, nobility or royalty – this type of residence fulfilled important administrative functions and the owner could use his manor as a hub from which to exert his power. The lord controlled and managed his landed estates from his seat and, to maintain his right and gain further wealth and prestige, often made sure he was also perceived as potent and affluent. A country residence usually had to provide a suitable practical and ceremonial setting for these purposes. English manors can serve as a good example of such a setup. Externally, a manor had to proclaim the wealth and status of its owner. This could be achieved by many means and the choice of building material was the usual starting point. However, the style of architecture, the size of the building and the paraphernalia used were stronger indicators of the importance, connections, affluence, sophistication and ambitions of the builder and his heirs. Adaptations of the newest architectural trends, glazed windows, noticeable chimney stacks and the conspicuous display of coats of arms combined all over Europe to create the desired effect. Interiors were supposed to match the splendid exterior and to echo the features advertised to the world outside. The layout of a manor house varied according to the customs of the inhabitants. For instance, due to ceremonial dining rituals and elaborate household ordinances, some notable English manors underwent a remarkable gradual development resulting not only in the specialisation of rooms but in their sometimes quite rigid and predictable positioning within the building. A typical late medieval layout would encompass a large rectangular hall with a dais for the lord's table at one end and with three arched doorways leading to the buttery, pantry and kitchen at the other end. To prevent fire and undesirable smells, the kitchen itself was situated at the end of the passage, often in a separate building. By and large, a country-house kitchen would be part of a complex of isolated outbuildings and provide food for a very large household. The bakery, the brewery and, if the climate allowed, the wine press were its main constituents (Fig. 26–29, 78, 79).

The typology of medieval and Renaissance houses is not straightforward. One of the major issues contributing to the uncertainty is the fact that architectural elements typical of high-status medieval architecture were frequently imitated and utilised as mostly non-functional status symbols in houses of lesser eminence. On the other hand, Renaissance buildings initially commissioned by patricians provided blueprints for features adopted by their social superiors. The first process can be illustrated by constituents of medieval castle architecture, the second by Florentine palazzi and later Renaissance residences.

Castle towers, initially utilitarian structures for spotting approaching enemies at a considerable distance, in time became symbolic indicators of chivalry, supremacy, power and wealth. As conspicuous emblems of authority, towers similar to the ones erected on castles were also constructed by members of other classes, mainly the landed gentry or wealthy merchants aiming to flaunt their means and indicate their social ambitions. Towers were a familiar feature in many European towns and were often used as lodgings. Usually of stone and hence durable and secure, they were also frequently employed for the protection of personal possessions and merchandise. One of the most striking examples of a still extant accumulation of towers in an urban context is the historic centre of the Italian town of San Gimignano, where rival families competed with

[27]
Calendar page for December. A kitchen and a bakery on a country estate.

Simon Bening and workshop, Book of Hours (Golf Book), Bruges, probably early 1540s; British Library, Add. MS 24098, fol. 29 v

[28]
Calendar page for August.
Harvesting grapes and making wine
on an Italian country estate, with
vine-trellis in the background.

Attributed to Giovanni Boccardi, Book of
Hours (The Hours of Laudomia de' Medici),
Florence, c. 1502; British Library, Yates
Thompson MS 30, fol. 8

[29]
Calendar page for October. Flemish
manor house or castle complex with
a winepress.

Simon Bening and workshop, Book of
Hours (Golf Book), Bruges, probably early
1540s; British Library, Add. MS 24098,
fol. 27 v

one another in building these imposing edifices on narrow plots of land and in a very confined area restricted by the medieval town walls. Other elements typical of high and late medieval castle architecture, such as moats, drawbridges, portcullises, arrow slits and battlements, were also frequently borrowed by builders of later medieval or Renaissance houses of non-defensive character (Fig. 30). The inclusion of such features of aristocratic and chivalric origins was often a way of adding an aura of splendour and romance to a new house that was chiefly residential and commissioned by a newcomer striving for grandeur. Bodiam Castle in East Sussex can serve as an example of this partly symbolic treatment of architecture. Built by Sir Edward Dalyngrigge in the late fourteenth century, it appears designed to provide protection from invaders. The building displays elements of a traditional curtain-wall castle. However, its numerous defensive weaknesses are an indication of its primarily manorial origin and use. Although all houses were meant to give some level of security to their inhabitants, only genuine castles could be defended in times of a serious conflict. Obviously, many other types of houses, such as English or Flemish medieval fortified manors or Italian Renaissance palaces, also had a partially protective purpose and could withstand a minor turmoil (Fig. 14, 22). As window openings compromised security, the lower floors of buildings constructed in unstable times and unsafe vicinities tended to have fewer and smaller window openings, which were almost always fitted with iron grilles (Fig. 14). The Palazzo Medici, a Florentine patrician townhouse commissioned in the 1440s by Cosimo de' Medici, the *de facto* ruler of Florence, and designed probably by Michelozzo, illustrates this practice well. It also gives an example of battlements, clearly adapted from castle architecture, which were used to crown the garden wall behind the palace. Built in the mid-fifteenth century in a then new architectural style and constructed around a symmetrical central arcaded courtyard, the Palazzo Medici became a celebrated precursor of numerous similar Renaissance houses both in Tuscany and beyond. This type of townhouse and its style was quickly replicated in other Florentine fifteenth-century patrician buildings, such as the Palazzo Rucellai and the Palazzo Strozzi. In Urbino it was adapted for the ducal palace of Federico da Montefeltro, and in Pienza for a house of Pope Pius II. Abroad, the type was modified to suit regional traditions and climates, for instance in Bruges at the Hof Bladelin, a townhouse originally built in the Gothic style in the 1450s by Pieter Bladelin, a treasurer of the Order of the Golden Fleece. About two decades later, the house was altered and Renaissance elements were introduced by the subsequent Florentine owners, the Medici family, and Tommaso Portinari, a manager of the Bruges branch of the Medici bank and a councillor to the Duke of Burgundy, Charles the Bold. The architectural elements, the characteristic decoration style and some of the layout components (though not necessarily the shape and proportions) of fifteenth-century Florentine Renaissance palazzi were also accepted throughout Europe in contemporary buildings of a much higher status than their townhouse forerunners. Popularised by humanist patrons, Italian artists and architects and the dissemination of printed designs, aspects of Italian Renaissance style found their way into European ducal and royal residences. Works carried out in the first half of the sixteenth century for the English King Henry VIII at Whitehall Palace and Hampton Court, for the French King François I at his Fontainebleau Palace and for the Polish King Zygmunt Stary at Wawel, the royal castle in Kraków, illustrate this development. The nobility and middle classes followed their example. Building exteriors (arcaded courtyards, porticos, window surrounds) and interiors (ceilings, floors, walls, chimneypieces) were transformed in line with the new Renaissance trend, and so were furniture and other objects of domestic use.

[30]
Apothecary's shop. Ceramic and metal jars with medicine and cosmetics are placed on the shelves. Note the red door with decorative iron bands and a doorknocker. The sturdy gate, turrets, walls and battlements are elements of castle architecture.

Mattheus Platearius, *Circa instans* (trans. into French), Amiens, first quarter of the 14th century; British Library, Sloane MS 1977, fol. 49 v

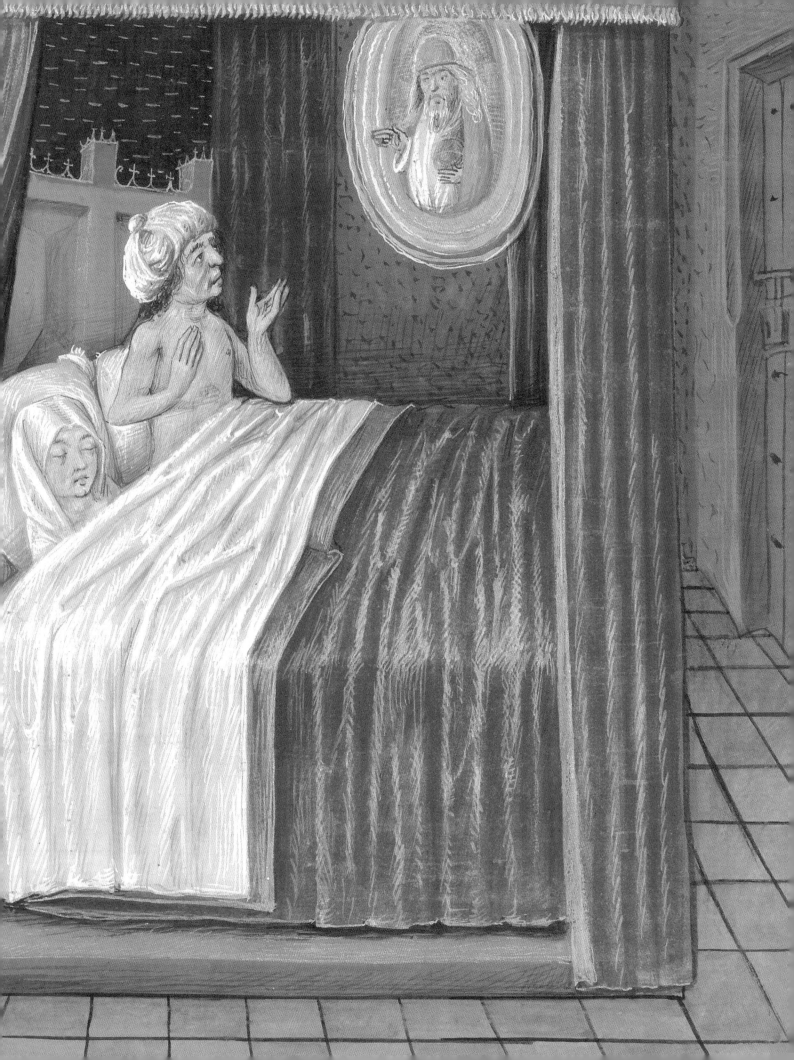

III
PROVIDING A SAFE HAVEN

Entrance doors had a vital function in medieval and Renaissance buildings. To a much greater extent than nowadays, and especially in the frequent times of military conflict and civil unrest, they had to provide enhanced security and protection for the inhabitants. In castles and other buildings with a defensive function, reinforced doors and stairs leading up to them were often a part of a system of defences that could include a moat, a drawbridge and a portcullis.

Windows, just like doors, needed to provide security and protect from the elements. As windows had to let in light, their history includes not only such elements as the forms of window openings but also shutters, iron grilles, glazing and other window inserts.

At the same time, doors and windows were used as an important site for exterior and interior decoration. They were constructed and decorated according to successive architectural styles, and they are among the main indicators providing information on the history of a building.

1. Doors and Stairs

EXTERNAL DOORS AND DOORWAYS: CONSTRUCTION AND DECORATION

Following the example of very ornate ecclesiastical sculpted doorways, their counterparts in secular buildings – castles, palaces and townhouses built for display – were also elaborately designed and executed. Medieval doorways at first had rounded Romanesque arches, later pointed Gothic, then rounded or straight Renaissance door heads with architraves. Door surrounds were often decorated with columns and topped by Romanesque tympanums and porticos, Gothic arches or hood mouldings (bands of stonework) and Renaissance cornicing and pediments. Projecting surrounds, such as porches or hood mouldings, not only decorated entrances but also protected them from the elements (Fig. 30, 97).

External doors were constructed of one or two timber leaves. Paired doors were considered to be grander and were customarily installed in entrances to buildings rather than in their interior. Medieval domestic doors were usually constructed from vertical boards of strong timber. These were normally kept together and reinforced by horizontal and

[31]
Amaram and his wife in their bedroom. Note the large lock on the door.

Master of Edward IV, Vincent of Beauvais, *Le miroir historial* (*Speculum historiale*, trans. into French by Jean de Vignay), Book 3, Bruges, *c.* 1479–*c.* 1480; British Library, Royal MS 14 E I, fol. 77

diagonal planks and by iron fastenings. The fastenings were usually connected to the door's hinges. At first, iron fastenings were relatively modest and formed by splitting plain iron bands into two scrolls. In time, they became very elaborate and gradually covered doors with beautiful, intricate geometric or floral patterns. Strong nails held the door boards together and, if arranged neatly, embellished them. This fashion survived till the Renaissance. Many examples of medieval doors of this type still exist, particularly in Germany. In the UK a beautiful late fourteenth-century example covered with complicated iron scrollwork can be seen at Merton College in Oxford. In Kraków, many of the surviving typical sixteenth-century entrance doors to university and church buildings or townhouses are coated with iron sheets, braced with nets of diamond-shaped iron bands and embossed with decorative nails. When not covered with functional ironwork decoration, late medieval doors could be carved with Gothic tracery, as on the entrance door to the Divinity School in the Bodleian Library in Oxford. Renaissance door decoration was influenced by classical design, and coffering such as that on the fifteenth-century Florentine Palazzo Rucellai became very popular.

Entrance doors could be bolted with a thick timber plank or an iron bar from the inside of the house. Less secure but more convenient were door locks, which had been in use since Antiquity. The door lock mechanism was encased in an iron box and attached to the door (Fig. 30, 31, 32, 77). Early door handles were very fragile. If attached to the lock, they were not usually meant to be used to open the door itself, but solely to release the locking mechanism. The doors had to be pulled open by means of sturdy doorknobs, or grips which sometimes, especially on external doors, were either paired with or doubled as doorknockers. These could be completely separate from the delicate door lock and frequently made from brass in the form of an animal head and a ring.

INTERNAL DOORS

Internal doors were constructed in the same way as entrance doors and could be lockable, though they were less sturdy and often more ornamental. Internal doorways copied the forms of their external counterparts. Door leaves could be decorated with ornaments such as Gothic carved tracery or Renaissance inlaid wood (*tarsie*) and coffering. Some trends changed quickly. For example, inlaid door panels were very popular in Italy in the first half of the fifteenth century but went out of fashion by *c.* 1500. Inlaid panels disappeared together with the profiled mouldings that framed them and were replaced by plain wood panels and carved mouldings (Fig. 33, 34).

To blend in with the surrounding decoration scheme, especially in richly frescoed rooms in Renaissance Italian high-status residences, door leaves could also be painted with a continuation of the mural design. For the same reason, additional fake doors could be painted on the wall, if this helped with balancing the overall classical and symmetrical design of such ornate interiors.

Some internal doorways, even if fitted with doors, could have *portières*: pieces of fabric that had the same purpose and looked very much like today's window-curtains or blinds and would be matched to the wall decoration and other fittings. *Portières* in high-status residences could even be of costly tapestry. Verdure tapestries, very popular as wall hangings, were also used in doorways. An example can be seen in the January calendar illumination from the Grimani Breviary and in the 1480s *Birth of St John the Baptist* fresco by Domenico Ghirlandaio in the Tornabuoni Chapel in Santa Maria Novella in Florence (Fig. 126).

[32]
Garden of Pleasure. Gardens were an important part of domestic life. As fountains were sometimes installed to regulate water pressure in conduits, it is possible that the buildings associated with this garden had running water. Also, note the sophisticated lock on the garden door and a key to it.
Master of the Prayer Books of around 1500, Guillaume de Lorris and Jean de Meun, *Roman de la rose*, Bruges, *c.* 1490–*c.* 1500; British Library, Harley MS 4425, fol. 12 v

[33]
St Matthew writing. The door and the ceiling are panelled in a matching style. The tapestry (or mural?) at the back of the room is decorated with a design typical of fifteenth-century textiles. Note the comfortable lectern.
Simon Marmion and workshop; cuttings from a Book of Hours, Valenciennes, late 1460s; British Library, Add. MS 71117, fol. C

[34]
The birth of Caesar in a Gothic bedchamber. The bedstead with silk velvet hanging is particularly impressive. The door is panelled with linenfold carving.
La grant hystoire Cesar (*Les faits des Romains*, with additional texts), Bruges, 1479; British Library, Royal MS 17 F II, fol. 9

[35]

A hall and a simple staircase in a palace. These illuminations of palace interiors (compare Fig. 100) come from a series of medieval sermons using chess as a metaphor for social structure. This one shows a Roman emperor and his wife in a contemporary, high-status medieval Italian interior.

Jacobus de Cessolis, *De ludo scachorum*, Venice? *c.* 1400?; British Library, Add. MS 15685, fol. 92 v

[36]

Pentecost in a Flemish interior. The illumination is dominated by a stone staircase along the back wall of a hall, and by the imposing fireplace. The timber ceiling is vaulted and the arched windows are glazed. A clock decorates the otherwise bare, grey walls.

Master of the David Scenes in the Grimani Breviary, Book of Hours, Flanders, beginning 16th century; Bodleian Library, University of Oxford, MS Douce 256, fol. 36 v

STAIRS, STAIRCASES AND VESTIBULES

In defensive medieval buildings, such as the keep of the Tower of London (the White Tower) and other contemporary castles, the main entrance doorway was placed very high above ground level. Usually it was reached by narrow stairs. Timber stairs were especially practical as they could be quickly removed in times of danger. In medieval buildings, internal timber stairs, probably for the same reason, were also very utilitarian, modest, narrow and placed directly next to the walls. Such fixtures were essentially an upmarket version of a ladder, such as was used instead of stairs in poor dwellings and rarely survive. Medieval stone stairs were also very narrow. Often built into turrets, they formed spiral staircases, which were secure and easy to defend (Fig. 35, 36, 50).

In late medieval and Renaissance northern Europe, doorways and staircases were sometimes enclosed in timber vestibules. These, fitted with doors, provided additional security and privacy and protected from draughts. They were often covered with fashionable carving to complement the appearance of the room. Contemporary depictions of such vestibules can be seen in several late fifteenth-century French and early sixteenth-century Flemish illuminations showing halls and studies in high-status interiors (Fig. 10, 37, 62, 70). A similar vestibule, originally from Tours in northern France, is in the collection of the Victoria and Albert Museum in London.

In Renaissance Italy, above all in non-defensive fifteenth-century buildings, stairs underwent a further development. At first

widened, they were later also moved away from walls and, particularly when executed in stone, gained a ceremonial and decorative function. At the same time, turned or carved balusters were introduced as an enhancement. This new type of much grander stairs and staircases was adopted and became popular in the rest of Europe in the sixteenth century. Examples of such wider staircases can be seen in Florence, for instance the mid-fifteenth-century stairs in the Palazzo Medici, and in the mid-sixteenth-century staircase, designed by Michelangelo and built by Ammannati, that leads up to the Biblioteca Medicea Laurenziana.

2.Windows

WINDOW FORMS

Windows, like doors, followed successive architectural styles and, as well as being functional, served to decorate façades and building interiors.

A simple rectangle has always been the most widespread window shape. It existed in all types of European civic and private buildings of all classes, whether ecclesiastical or secular, of stone or of timber.

The most basic medieval and Renaissance windows were found in peasant houses. They were simply an unprotected and unadorned opening in a wall. Illuminations show numerous examples of how their appearance depended on the construction of the house: tiny rectangular openings in Italian stone farmhouses, or a slightly broader opening, divided by one or more wooden posts but otherwise bare, in Flemish half-timber wattle-and-daub buildings (Fig. 12, 25, 27, 38, 39).

A more sophisticated version of the simple window opening was a round marigold window. These were often fitted in churches or other ecclesiastical or profane high-status buildings and developed into complex rose windows (Fig. 12, 14, 46, 63).

However, the characteristic Romanesque and Gothic windows, instantly recognisable as medieval, had arched tops, the former rounded, the latter pointed. They were the most fashionable and preferred type of apertures in middle- and high-status secular and sacred buildings. The window surrounds could be made either of stone or of timber. Single arched window openings were frequently put together in groups of two, three

[38]
Calendar page for November. Barns and farm buildings on a country estate.

Simon Bening and workshop, Book of Hours (Golf Book), Bruges, probably early 1540s; British Library, Add. MS 24098, fol. 28 v

[39]
St Matthew writing in his study. Note the simple unglazed window with rustic shutters.

Book of Hours, France (Amiens), between 1430 and 1440; British Library, Add. MS 31835, fol. 16 v

or sometimes more (Fig. 14, 40, 41, 56, 93, 94, 95, 100). Such window clusters were very similar to the simple window openings in half-timbered buildings, but much more decorative. Their individual openings (lights) were separated by colonettes. These pillars fulfilled an important structural function but, being topped with capitals and often decoratively carved, they also enhanced the window's appearance. Beautiful examples of such windows can be seen in houses located on the Grand Canal in Venice.

Romanesque window arches were miniature versions of other architectural arches of the time and echoed the austere elegance of the half-round arched openings of Romanesque portals. Generally, Romanesque arched windows were very small and let in little light. If they were clustered, the pillars separating their individual openings had a very large diameter.

Gothic windows first appeared in buildings at the end of the twelfth century. The style originated in France and was rapidly adopted in other European countries. Gothic architecture and its new pointed arches made use of new building technologies, which allowed for taller buildings and for larger door and window openings. As the style developed, Gothic windows gradually grew larger, which resulted in interiors filled with considerably more light than those of previous periods. Window arches became more and more elaborate and were decorated with very intricate and increasingly sophisticated and spectacular tracery (Fig. 9, 56, 93, 94, 100).

From the late fourteenth century, in domestic buildings, casement windows gradually replaced the typically Gothic windows with pointed arches. They became very fashionable and have been prevalent in Europe since the Renaissance. The new casement windows were rectangular, typically large, and divided into two, four or sometimes more openings, which were also rectangular and grouped in pairs. The individual openings forming a casement window were separated by vertical posts (mullions) and horizontal crossbars (transoms), an essentially modern and still popular window form. This new development was associated with increased and systematic use of glass inserts in

[40]
The figure of Hagiography showing books to a pilgrim. The room is lit by a row of round-arched windows. The design of the lecterns is typical of fifteenth-century library spaces.

John Lydgate, *The Pilgrimage of the Life of Man*, England (West Suffolk?), *c.* 1430–50; British Library, Cotton Tiberius MS A. VII, fol. 91 v

[41]
The interior of a counting house. Ornamental, round-arched biforate windows pierce the façade at regular intervals.

Master of the Cocharelli Codex, Cocharelli, *Treatise on the Vices*, Genoa, *c.* 1330–*c.* 1340; British Library, Add. MS 27695, fol. 7 v

[42]
Aristotle instructing Alexander. In noble households children were taught at home by eminent scholars. A special schoolroom or the father's study could have been used for this purpose. Note the casement window, which became popular in the late fourteenth century.

Attributed to the Master of the Royal Alexander, *Le Livre et le vraye hystoire du bon roy Alixandre* (*Historia de proelis*, trans. into French), Paris, *c.* 1420; British Library, Royal MS 20 B XX, fol. 10 v

windows (Fig. 1, 18, 21, 42, 43, 46, 48, 50, 52, 58, 77, 88, 91, 104, 107, 118, 131, 135, 138).

The Gothic pointed arch style was universal in northern Europe until as late as the sixteenth century. In southern Europe, however, especially in most Italian city states, it was less widespread, and there was a faster adoption of Renaissance forms with round-arched or horizontal tops, based on local antique architecture and its reinterpretation. As we see in the illumination depicting it, the Palazzo Medici – a pioneering house in the city that initiated the Renaissance style – also included the latest development in the form of its windows. Single round-arched windows were quite typical at that time for Florentine houses, but the large biforate windows of this palazzo, consisting of two round-arched openings, have a Renaissance form and resemble in design, if not in size, smaller high-status biforate Romanesque windows (Fig. 14).

Finally, one has to bear in mind that technical and intellectual development, the function of a building, and changes in fashion were not always the main factors influencing the appearance of windows. For instance, their size largely depended on regional differences in weather conditions. Large windows catch more light but are not always desirable: smaller windows have always been more practical in very hot or very cold climates.

Medieval and Renaissance windows were frequently depicted, but they are not only known from paintings, illuminations, woodcuts and etchings. Though they are often partially reconstructed, many complete windows of the period or fragments of their masonry, and even window glass and lead settings, have survived in extant buildings or have been excavated and can be seen in museums.

WOODEN SHUTTERS

Shutters could be installed on both glazed and unglazed windows. Unlike the fragile glazing, shutters were essential and their function was all-encompassing and multifarious. Although quite frequent in medieval churches and in royal and princely dwellings, glass was a luxury commodity in the Middle Ages and Renaissance, and therefore rare in lower-status domestic buildings until as late as the fourteenth century. As windows needed to be closed with less costly material, shutters and inserts made from wood were a much cheaper alternative, available to all. Small Romanesque windows were easy to cover with robust wooden shutters, which did not need hinges. These detached wooden boards could be placed on a window-sill and bolted firmly to the internal wall with a horizontal bar. Blocking a window in such a robust way effectively sheltered the inhabitants from the elements – drafts, wind and snow in the winter, rain and glaring sunlight in the summer – but also offered good protection from burglars at night and from the enemy in times of war. In fact small window openings were a necessity in medieval castles, which were defensive structures.

With time, shutters acquired hinges and became increasingly complex and technologically advanced. Some simple attached wooden shutters opened horizontally. They consisted of undivided, rigid wooden boards and could be hinged to the top or fastened to the bottom of a window. It seems likely that their popularity was limited and illuminations show them very infrequently and unclearly. Several Flemish and French fourteenth- and fifteenth-century illuminations depict castles or houses with top-hinged

[43]
The translator Simon de Hesdin at work. This study is bare and looks rather uncomfortable but is nevertheless charming. It is furnished with a lectern and a long bench running along the walls. The window is partially glazed, with multi-coloured glass in its upper part. A wooden lattice in the lower section provides privacy. The shutters consist of several parts, which can be opened or closed independently. The cupboards are quite interesting: two are in the wall niches and have doors decorated with Flemish linenfold panelling. Another cupboard, or a simple open shelving unit, is fixed to the wall. The undecorated plastered walls seem to be scratched and neglected. The inscription reads 'Je suis bien/Toudis Joieulx/1479'. See also page 6.

Master of the White Inscriptions, *Valerius Maximus, Facta et dicta memorabilia* (translated by Simon de Hesdin and Nicholas de Gonesse), Bruges, 1479; British Library, Royal MS 18 E III, fol. 24

shutters opening outwards and propped up by means of rods or wedges (*Romance of Alexander*, Oxford University, Bodleian Library, MS Bodl. 264, Pt. 1, fol. 20 verso). Other horizontal shutters could be attached to ground floor windowsills and opened outwards to form a table or a counter. Some fifteenth- and sixteenth-century European illuminations show them, somewhat sketchily, in association with lower-status establishments: workshops, shops, market stalls or taverns (*Des profits ruraux des champs*, British Library, Add. MS 19720, fol. 80). Finally, one of the best-known fifteenth-century Flemish panel paintings, the Mérode Altarpiece by the Flémalle Master, depicts very precisely a horizontal shutter installed, probably not coincidentally, in an unglazed window of St Joseph's workshop. It is hinged above the window, opened inwards and kept in place by a simple catch attached to the ceiling.

The shutters most frequently illustrated, seen on countless illuminations, were the type hinged vertically and opening to the inside of the room, and which could be locked when closed. Depending on the size of the window, they could still consist of one single board but larger windows had two-leaved shutters. These were often further divided into smaller leaves, which were hinged independently to provide flexibility. Such a construction enabled one to open and close various parts of the shutters independently (Fig. 8, 11, 18, 39, 42, 43, 45, 48, 59, 61, 62, 75, 84, 88, 104, 107, 118, 135).

IRON GRILLES

Found throughout Europe and still in use today, fixed iron grilles were another window safety feature. These were most frequently installed on the ground floor and were often unaccompanied by glazing, shutters or other window covers (Fig. 14, 35, 98). In exceptional settings, such as the French royal bedroom depicted in Christine de Pizan's works, a window could be fitted with all three features. The illumination showing it was painted when both the casement form of the window and its glazed movable leaves must have been a novelty (Fig. 8, 88, 135).

GLASS AND OTHER WINDOW INSERTS

Although not unknown in Romanesque windows, the considerable practical advantages of glass first became more apparent in Gothic buildings. Large Gothic windows, in spite of letting in more light, gave less protection from the elements than their much smaller Romanesque predecessors and glass inserts were an obvious solution to the problem (Fig. 9, 45, 56, 94).

Glass used for medieval and Renaissance window panes or glazed inserts was made of round and thick bull's-eye glass pieces, or of thinner rectangular glass quarrels, which were small and flat, either lozenge-shaped or narrow. Both types of window glass were produced and used both north and south of the Alps, though French and English glass was allegedly more transparent than its Venetian counterpart. Probably for both practical and aesthetic reasons, one normally chose glass coming from a single production centre rather than mixing different types of glass in one window pane. The glass pieces themselves looked pretty similar and were constructed alike everywhere in Europe. Regardless of its shape, each piece of glass was mounted in a separate lead setting, and these were soldered together to construct a window pane. The spaces created by mounting roundels of glass next to one another were filled with small angular glass pieces which were often coloured (Fig. 44, 77). The small flat rhomboid-shaped glass pieces fitted one another snugly and did not need any internal 'fillers'. Their edges were clipped to create a rectangular window pane which was sometimes framed by a thin band of flat, coloured glass strips. The colours usually preferred for such frames were blue, green, yellow and red (Fig. 43, 50). Some of the more luxurious windows could be partially decorated with stained glass ornamentation, for which the favourite motif was the owner's coat of arms. Netherlandish panel paintings show

[44]
Bonaventure, a biographer of Francis of Assisi, in his study. The noticeable lack of room in this study is not an exaggeration. Italian Renaissance studies were often very well equipped and furnished but designed to fit in tiny, personal spaces. Note bookshelves fitted high above a bull's-eye glass window and carved desk.

Attributed to Stefano Lunetti, Bonaventure, *Legend and Life of Francis of Assisi (with Miracles)*, Florence, 1504; British Library, Harley MS 3229, fol. 26

this fashion frequently (for instance, in Memling's diptych of Maarten Nieuwenhove, dated 1487 and now in the Memlingmuseum, Sint-Janshospitaal, Bruges, or the above mentioned Master of Flémalle's Mérode Altarpiece). Some illuminated manuscripts also depict such windows (Fig. 45, 46).

Finished glass panes could be either inserted directly into a window opening or set into a movable wooden frame. Whether fixed or movable, the glass panes in their pliable lead mounts were very fragile and had to be reinforced with thin but strong horizontal iron bars. Attached to the inside or outside of the glass pane, they supported it, gave additional stability and protected it from gusts of wind (Fig. 8, 42, 46, 48).

Glass was not only very expensive but also difficult to fit into arched windows, especially those that were decorated with elaborate tracery. For these reasons, many windows remained either unglazed or were glazed only partially. Nevertheless, some windows did get completely glazed with permanently fixed glass inserts, though these were not always convenient. They did not allow one to open the window to air the room or to see outside, as most types of early glass were translucent but not transparent. To be able to do both, one needed to glaze a movable window frame and not the surround of the window opening. The complicated shape of the decoratively carved parts of the arched windows presented an almost impossible challenge to anyone wishing to construct a frame that would be sturdy enough to hold the glass safely and fit

[45]
John, Duke of Bedford, praying to his patron saint. Note the stained glass roundels in the windows depicting the duke's coat of arms.

The Bedford Master, Book of Hours (The Bedford Hours), Paris, c. 1423–30; British Library, Add. MS 18850, fol. 256 v

[46]
Presentation scene. Charles Pineau is presenting the book to Jean de Laval, baron de Chateaubriant, in an exquisite French Renaissance interior. Jean de Laval is sitting on an elaborate settle, and behind him is a private chapel. The windows are fully glazed and are decorated with stained glass inserts bearing his coat of arms.

In the style of Jean Pichore, *Explication des actes des apôtres*, Paris, c. 1510; British Library, Harley MS 4393, fol. 2 v

tightly, yet not spoil the aesthetic appeal of the arch. Windows were therefore 'divided' into separate zones, which could have various types of inserts. As movable window inserts could be more securely fitted into rectangular openings, sometimes the top part of an arched window was glazed permanently and a movable glazed frame consisting of rectangular lights was inserted into the lower part of the window (Fig. 88). Frames for window inserts were made of wood, which could be painted or even gilded. Movable glazed frames were suspended from strong hinges on the inside of the window aperture, opened inwards and could be locked to keep the closed glazed leaves steady.

Alternatively, the bottom lights of such windows could be left unglazed or fitted with a movable rectangular frame holding a cheaper variety of filling. Such an insert was normally intended to exclude draughts and provide privacy and could be made from other translucent materials, such as oiled linen. Wooden grilles or lattices, which allowed one to see outside but obscured the view into the room, were also very popular (Fig. 43).

[47]
Annunciation scene in a Tuscan Renaissance *palazzo* courtyard. This is a rare depiction of typically Italian fabric window inserts (*impannate*) in an illumination. A water-cistern opening is visible in the middle of the yard. Renaissance symmetrical internal courtyards were first built in Florence in the 1450s. Probably designed by Michelozzo, the Palazzo Medici was a precursor of these.

Attributed to Attavante degli Attavanti, Book of Hours, Florence, *c.* 1490; Fitzwilliam Museum, University of Cambridge, MS 154, fol. 13 v

Frames fitted with cheaper types of material were normally not hinged but inserted snugly into the bottom part of the window surround.

Descriptions, or short notes, of glazed windows are found in archival sources though they are not very detailed. When glass was still rare in domestic interiors, inventories sometimes mention the fact that some windows were glazed. For instance, there is a note about two glazed windows in a house in Bologna in 1335. Accounts also contribute to knowledge in this area. For example they document a Venetian glazier who imported glass to Ferrara, where he installed glass into windows in the 1440s. Travellers' journals can also be useful here, though these normally concentrate on descriptions of windows of high aesthetic value, like those decorated with stained glass, which obviously was even more costly, of far greater rarity than plain glass, and used only in very high-status buildings.

[48]
Fortune approaching Boccaccio. Note the spectacular partially glazed window with shutters and a comfortable seat, beamed ceiling, bare walls and stone-tiled floor. A typically Flemish city can be seen in the background.

Master of the Getty Froissart, Giovanni Boccaccio, *Des cas des ruynes des nobles hommes et femmes* (*De casibus virorum illustrium*, trans. into French by Laurent de Premierfait), Bruges, *c.* 1479–*c.* 1480; British Library, Royal MS 14 E V, fol. 291

TEXTILE *IMPANNATE*

Impannate were window covers used in warmer climates. Typical in Italy, they were inserted into windows as a practical cross between glazing and blinds. *Impannate* were made of textiles drenched with oil and stretched over a wooden frame. Divided into horizontal sections, they were hinged and opened horizontally outwards by means of cords. They let in some light and could cover either the entire window opening or a portion of it (Fig. 47).

INTERNAL WALL WINDOW FEATURES: SPLAYING AND SEATS

In order to let more light into rooms than the combination of a small opening and thick stone walls allowed, walls could be angled, or splayed, to make the window opening much wider on the inside of the building than on the outside (Fig. 3, 33, 50, 61, 118, 136). To make use of all the available light, many medieval windows were flanked by two window seats (Fig. 48). Such seats were used for reading, sewing and playing board games and for other activities requiring light. To increase comfort, window seats were often covered with cushions. They were also adorned with wall hangings or painted to match the decorative scheme of the room. Renaissance windows continued to have window seats, and their form remained mostly unchanged, though novelty benches, like the one in the Gonzaga Hours, were also introduced (Fig. 49).

[49]
The birth of St John the Baptist in a Renaissance bedroom. Note the window bench providing access to natural light. A bath for the baby is being prepared and water warmed up and poured into a large metal basin similar to the wine cooler in Fig. 92. The cat is sitting in a very unusually shaped cradle.

Vincenzo Raimondi, Book of Hours (Hours of Eleonora Ippolita Gonzaga), Italy, Urbino or Mantua?, 1527 or earlier; Bodleian Library, University of Oxford, MS Douce 29, fol. 23 v

EXTERNAL WALL WINDOW FEATURES: HOOD MOULDINGS AND HORIZONTAL RODS

Late medieval and Renaissance northern European external walls were embellished with raised masonry bands surrounding the heads of windows, called hood mouldings. These were very decorative but their primary function was diversion of rain from window openings.

Another widespread window feature, mainly in Italy, was the use of horizontal rods. Attached to the façade of buildings, at about half-height on a row of windows, they could be used in a variety of ways: for suspending decorative banners at times of festivities, for hanging bird cages, or even for airing textiles. Although mainly used in Italy, this device was not unknown in northern Europe. Cities with Italian mercantile communities, such as Bruges, occasionally had rods on exteriors of their buildings. These are sometimes documented on Flemish illuminations showing fifteenth- and sixteenth-century cityscapes (for example, in University of Oxford, Bodleian Library, MS Liturg. 58, fol. 116 verso).

IV
WITHIN THE FOUR WALLS

Floors, walls and ceilings had a vital structural, load-bearing function in buildings and their appearance depended predominantly on the type of their construction.

Medieval and Renaissance farmhouses, which often consisted of one storey, frequently had primitive earthen floors. These could be cobbled and covered with rushes or simple rush matting. More affluent households had timber, stone, brick or ceramic floors supplemented by matting or carpets.

Although walls in less well-off houses were often left bare and, perhaps apart from the usual plaster and whitewash, unadorned, those in prosperous households provided one of the main interior surfaces for sometimes flamboyant display of the occupants' taste, sophistication and wealth.

Ceilings were made of wood or masonry. Timber ceilings were beamed – opened to the roof or flat – or vaulted. Masonry ceilings were vaulted. As they supported floors or roofs above them, their construction had to be very sturdy. Nevertheless they were also often extremely decorative and could be painted, panelled and coffered.

1. Floors

TIMBER
Wood was a widely used floor material both in high-status residences and in unprivileged medieval and Renaissance dwellings across Europe. It would typically be used on upper floors, which could not bear the weight of brick, stone or ceramics, the heavy floor coverings normally installed on ground floors. Above all, numerous Flemish miniatures record timber floors in all types of interiors ranging from the humblest to the most affluent (Fig. 1, 5, 10, 50, 58, 97, 140).

BRICK AND CERAMICS
Although surviving wooden floors dating back to the Middle Ages and the Renaissance are rare, many elements of contemporary brick, ceramic and stone floors still exist. The best examples tend to come from ecclesiastical contexts rather than domestic. Salisbury cathedral has one of the best medieval tiled floors surviving in situ, and the British Museum has a very good collection of medieval floor tiles from various sites. Visual

[50]
Death of Aristobulus and the murder of Antigonus. In this bedroom the wooden floor is combined with a brick hearth shaped around the fireplace. A silk coverlet, probably filled with cotton or wool, is placed on the bed.

Master of the Soane Josephus; Chronique de Baudouin d'Avennes (L'histoire tripartite, Le trésor de sapience), Flanders, Bruges?, between 1473 (written) and *c.* 1480 (illuminated); British Library, Royal MS 18 E. V, fol. 263

53

resources also show a multitude of such floors.

Brick floors were very common on ground floors of all types of houses. These consisted of thin floor bricks, which were often arranged in various decorative patterns, such as the herringbone, which was popular throughout Europe, especially in fifteenth-century Flanders and Italy (Fig. 50).

Ceramic tiles were a more upmarket variant of a brick floor. Typical medieval north European ornamental tiles were rectangular, reddish-brown and decorated with a white pattern. They were produced in moulds and could be glazed. The ornamental design was stamped into the tiles, and then filled with white slip. The most widespread patterns were usually geometric. As in other domestic interior decoration of that period, flora, fauna, heraldry and personal emblems were also universally used on tiles. Fifteenth- and sixteenth-century tiles, especially in northern Europe, could be covered in green glaze (Fig. 3, 8, 9, 39, 45, 51, 56, 61, 76, 88, 94, 104).

High-status Spanish *cuenca* and Italian maiolica (tin-glazed earthenware) tiles from the late Middle Ages and the Renaissance, decorated in vibrant colours, are difficult to find and to identify with certainty in illuminations (Fig. 131). Most maiolica and *cuenca* floors are known from Italian and Spanish ecclesiastical buildings respectively, but they were also used in domestic interiors. Both types of ceramic tiles were expensive and fragile but nevertheless used not only locally but exported across Europe. They were status symbols, as only the richest echelons of society could afford them. Imported from Seville, *cuenca* tiles were especially popular in affluent late Gothic and Renaissance Netherlandish interiors. As implied by Filarete in his *Trattato dell'architettura* or *Libro architettonico* (manuscript of *c.* 1465), one of the first fifteenth-century tin-glazed pavements, by a Florentine workshop of Luca della Robbia, was installed in a small but luxurious study (*studietto*) on the first floor (*piano nobile*) of Cosimo de' Medici's Palazzo Medici, later the residence also of his son Piero and his grandson Lorenzo. It seems to have inspired similar pavements, such as Andrea della Robbia's floor made up of hexagonal tiles in the San Lorenzo Chapel in the collegiate church at Empoli. Isabella d'Este, a prolific Renaissance patron of the arts and the wife of Francesco II Gonzaga, Marquess of Mantua, also had her splendid study (*studiolo*) fitted with a tin-glazed floor consisting of Pesaro ceramic tiles. We know from Isabella's household correspondence of 1494 that tiles were not only decorative but also practical, as they were supposed to stop rodents from burrowing under floor boards. Mice and rats were a persistent problem in even the highest-status houses. There are many depictions of mice in interiors, sometimes shown together with cats, which were kept both as pets and as rodent hunters (Fig. 5). Isabella d'Este was keen on keeping Syrian cats to deal with her vermin problem. Maiolica floors were also sought after in northern Europe, especially once Italian craftsmen started to make tin-glazed tiles and other household objects in Antwerp. Sixteenth-century maiolica and *cuenca* tiles were exported as far north as England. Both types survive at the Vyne, a splendid Tudor country seat remodelled by William Sandys, Henry VIII's Lord Chamberlain.

Finally, mention has to be made of *terrazzo* pavements, which were typical for Venetian Renaissance *palazzi*. Such floors were made of crushed brick and ceramic. Mixed with pulverised stone, compacted, levelled, dyed red and covered with linseed oil, they were durable, easy to clean and attractive enough to be installed in formal rooms. Venetian craftsmen sometimes installed them beyond Venice, for instance in Isabella d'Este's apartments in Mantua.

STONE

Stone tiles were an alternative to both brick and ceramic tiles and some floors combined all of these materials. Stone floors were installed in European houses of all classes. Cheaper, locally quarried stone was fitted in humbler dwellings, while more expensive, often imported and better-quality stone such as marble was reserved for important and affluent residences. Reflecting the differ-ences in its aesthetic value and quality, stone was cut into many shapes and arranged into a multitude of simple patterns or more sophisticated mosaics. Marble floors were more prevalent in Italy than elsewhere, and so were decorative mosaic stone floors. The art of laying mosaics had been known there since Antiquity and survived through the Middle Ages to the Renaissance. Such luxurious floors consisted of very small rectangular pieces of stone in various colours, skilfully laid to form intricate geometric patterns. Illumina-tions often show floors covered with mosaics, though it is sometimes difficult to tell the difference between representations of ceramic and stone floors (Fig. 31, 33, 37, 43, 46, 47, 48, 49, 51, 59, 62, 66, 72, 86, 103, 106, 107, 110, 116–18, 134, 136, 137).

Cosmati pavements are not easily identifiable in illuminations, and seem to be underrepresented. These inlaid floorings, Italian in origin and related to stone mosaics, consisted of *opus sectile,* cut stone and glass pieces of varying shapes. The pieces of stone and glass were inserted into stone matrices and, with them, formed very complex abstract patterns. Such pavements were much admired in the Middle Ages and were mainly applied in prominent ecclesiastical sites. They were named after the Cosmati family of artisans, who executed this type of pavement in Rome from the end of the twelfth to the end of the thirteenth century. One of the best examples outside Italy of such an opulent floor produced in this way is the 1268 pavement in front of the high altar of Westminster Abbey in London.

ADDITIONAL FLOOR COVERINGS

Various supplementary floor coverings were used for added insulation, comfort and decoration. These ranged from cheap materials such as loose rushes or straw, which

[51]
Institution of the Eucharist. Note the colourful tiled floor and various types of turned and joined seats. The x-framed seat is foldable.

Master of Mazarine 469, Book of Hours (The Hours of René d'Anjou, 1409–80, King of Naples), Paris, c. 1410; British Library, Egerton MS 1070, fol. 113

[52]
Women spinning at home. The floor
is carpeted wall to wall with typically
French matting. This type of floor
covering was also known in Tudor
English and Flemish interiors.

Attributed to Maître François, *Valerius
Maximus*, translated by Simon de Hesdin
and Nicholas de Gonesse, *Les Fais et les
dis des Romains et de autres gens*, Paris,
between 1473 and *c.* 1480; British Library,
Harley MS 4375, fol. 179

could be swept out and replaced regularly, through elaborate rush matting or wooden
platforms to very costly oriental carpets (Fig. 8, 13, 52, 76, 81, 87, 94, 114, 125, 126).

Sometimes a combination of various floor coverings was used. We can see such a
combination masterfully rendered in two illuminations, attributed to Barthélemy d'Eyck,
showing bedrooms in high-status buildings. One of them is a presentation scene in the
French translation of Boccaccio's *Théséide* and the other is the opening image of *Le Livre
du cœur d'amour épris* written by King René I of Anjou (both in the Österreichische
Nationalbibliothek, Vienna, respectively cod. 2617, fol. 14 verso, and cod. 2597, fol. 2).
The presentation scene takes place in a lady's room – probably in a castle, judging by
the view from her window. Here two large oriental rugs cover the floor all around the
bedstead, which stands in the corner of the room, and are laid on top of a floor paved
with terracotta tiles. The floor in the miniature in King René's manuscript is fitted with
wall-to-wall rush matting on which are laid two luxurious oriental carpets, one in front
of the king's bed, the other in front of his valet's mattress. This interior is possibly based
on King René's bedroom in one of his French castles, where he spent most of his life.

Imported oriental rugs were appreciated by the elite classes all over Europe. Rush
matting was known in other countries (such as England and Flanders), but it seems to
have been particularly typical of French homes. French illuminations repeatedly depict
such matting in bedrooms and halls. More public rooms and kitchens, often depicted
in the same manuscripts, appear however to have their tiled, cobbled or wooden floor
surfaces uncovered (Fig. 52, 81, 114).

Surprisingly, there are surviving examples of the perishable domestic floor coverings
that were so frequently depicted. Some very well-preserved rush matting, woven into
strips, was discovered under floorboards in Hampton Court Palace. It was fitted onto
plastered floorboards and probably dates from the time of Henry VIII.

2. Walls

LACK OF DECORATION?

Bare walls can clearly be seen in a February illumination from the Duc de Berry's Très Riches Heures showing a peasants' house (Fig. 53). However, many affluent households in northern Europe, chiefly in Flanders, also seem to have had undecorated walls. On these, in their upper portions, one can often recognise rows of hooks – an indication that the lack of decoration was deliberate and that costly hangings, probably Netherlandish tapestries, and not paint, which was much cheaper, were intended to serve as decoration.

It is sometimes difficult to determine if an illumination depicts a bare stone wall

[53]
Calendar page for February. A peasant family by the fire in their one-room cottage. A large bed or mattress, probably for all family members, is visible in the niche. Clothes are hung on rods fixed to the unadorned and bare walls. Note that in England early cottages had open hearths and that fireplaces do not appear in peasant houses until the sixteenth century. (However, they did have multiple rooms as early as the thirteenth century.) This is the first snowy winter landscape known in the history of art.

Limbourg brothers' workshop, Les Très Riches Heures de Jean de France, Duc de Berry, Franco-Netherlandish (Limbourg brothers active in France), 1411/12–16; Musée Condé, Chantilly, MS 65, fol. 2 v

or a plastered brick wall painted with a pattern imitating stone cladding, which was considered to be grander and more aesthetically pleasing than brick. Brick, more readily available than stone, was used in Flanders and in the rest of the Hanseatic region as the main building material. It was employed even in Burgundian ducal residences, and subsequently in English Tudor palaces, which emulated the Burgundian style. Brick was regarded as very versatile, decorative and suitable for exposed outside walls, but stone was considered to be more fitting for the interiors, so that brick walls were sometimes clad with stone or plastered and painted, often with a stone imitation (no doubt an extra insulation layer of plaster on the wall also contributed to comfort). Even genuine stone walls were sometimes plastered and painted with a masonry pattern: simulated ashlar stone would suggest larger, better-finished and more expensive blocks of stone than those actually used to build the wall. Examples of this practice are known from archaeological excavations, for instance in Bamberg, Germany, where such remains of painted plaster were found on the site of buildings belonging to the thirteenth-century Knights Templar (and later the Franciscans). Medieval masonry-patterned walls also survive in situ, for example in Selling church in Kent.

CHOICE OF MATERIALS, COLOURS AND DESIGNS

Across Europe, and particularly in Italy, the wealthy often ornately embellished the walls of their private residences, and many civic buildings were decorated in the same way.

Domestic walls could be painted with one simple block colour, with an array of patterns or, in high-status residences, even with spectacular figurative murals. Colours have always been ascribed individual properties. For instance, according to Pliny the Elder, for many centuries green had been considered to have a health-giving effect on people. Because of the belief in its positive qualities, green paint was often used in medieval domestic interior decoration (Fig. 91). It is also worth noting that pigments, as well as medicines and cosmetics, were often distributed by apothecaries and that in Florence painters belonged to the guild of doctors and apothecaries. For English inn decoration, red seems to have been favoured in the fifteenth century. In 1430–1 the Boar's Head Inn, on King Street in Westminster, was decorated with red lead and gold stencilling. Other contemporary secular and religious buildings in Europe were also decorated using similar techniques (colour and stencilled patterns) and painters carrying out such works were employed in cities such as Norwich, Ghent and Paris. Stencilled rosettes were very popular in the Middle Ages. A thirteenth-century stencilled rosette decoration in Selling church is applied to plastered walls painted with a masonry pattern. Each of the fake ashlar blocks is adorned with a stylised rosette accompanied by equally stylised tendrils and leaves.

Typical medieval European domestic wall paintings (and other embellishments) divided the wall surface into two or more distinct horizontal sections, which were often further visually broken up with vertical elements such as pilasters, either painted or real. Wall painting made use of the multifarious repertoire usual for interior decoration at this time: geometric designs, flora and fauna patterns, heraldry and figurative or historiated decoration were always fashionable (Fig. 54, 58, 101, 102). Medieval murals frequently imitated expensive textile or fur (especially miniver) wall hangings. A Renaissance equivalent of this type of simulation was usually painted marbling (Fig. 55). Other medieval patterns often included lozenges, chequers and stripes. Renaissance wall decorations, however, made use of newly excavated and rediscovered classical ornaments such as candelabras and grotesques. Candelabras were often applied as border decoration on columns, pilasters, portals and window surrounds. Fantastic grotesques, combining human, animal and floral forms, could also fill large surfaces. Such classical ornaments can also be seen in contemporary miniature borders, but walls decorated with them are rarely depicted in manuscripts (Fig. 46, 87, 137).

According to the means of the occupant, walls could also be adorned with art or decorative art objects: hangings, candleholders, mirrors or detached paintings and reliefs. Wall hangings were especially popular and used widely both for decoration and for insulation. They were made from wool, linen or even silk, or they could be leather, which was sometimes gilded. The most luxurious hangings were Netherlandish tapestries. Wood panelling, tiles and stone or marble cladding were also known in high-status residences, though these were much rarer and initially more popular in Italy, Spain and France respectively than in northern Europe. Wood panelling in particular became widely admired across Europe among the upper and middle classes, growing in popularity and becoming universal in the fifteenth century (Fig. 5, 8, 9, 15, 16, 46, 56, 57, 59–61, 97, 110, 116, 125, 131).

Some wall decorations, which could be executed in various media, created overall decoration schemes. Medieval schemes usually illustrated historical events, or episodes from the Bible or from medieval literature, while classical texts became fashionable in the Renaissance.

Appropriate decoration or narratives were often chosen to match the function of the rooms for which they were intended. For instance, bedrooms were likely to be painted with aesthetically pleasing, alluring images or amorous narratives, while heroic battle or tournament scenes would normally be more appropriate for banqueting halls or other formal reception rooms.

[55]
St Mark reading. He is using glasses. The wall behind him is either faced with marble or painted to imitate marble.

Jean Poyer (Poyet), Book of Hours (The Tilliot Hours), Tours, c. 1500; British Library, Yates Thompson MS 5, fol. 12

The choice of decoration for a domestic space was obviously a private decision but it did depend on tradition, which often went back to Antiquity and was reiterated and refined in the mid-fifteenth century by Leon Battista Alberti in his *De re aedificatoria*, in which he wrote not only about ideal architecture but also about interior decoration. *De re aedificatoria* was known in manuscript form to art and architecture patrons even before it was printed for the first time, in 1486 in Florence. Although various writings gave advice on suitable room decoration, the final choice was an individual matter. In private residences, such decisions were often made by the head of household.

The participation of inhabitants in the decoration of their houses seems to have been of great significance. It was not only people of moderate means who carefully thought about and planned these matters. Those of considerable social status, the nobility and royalty, were also actively involved in dialogue with craftsmen or artists. Their patronage of ecclesiastical architecture and art is more widely known and researched, but they also contributed in significant ways to secular building projects through the decisions they took and the commissions they placed for the interior decoration of their homes, as witnessed by a few surviving documents, such as contracts, or other written guidance for painters. Some written instructions are very individual and clearly refer to quite personal choices by the patron. For instance, a French contract of 1320 for new murals to be executed in a residence in Conflans near Paris contains extremely detailed instructions given to the painter Pierre de Bruxelles by Countess Mahaut d'Artois. The murals were to decorate a gallery and were to depict the deeds of the patroness's crusader father and of other knights accompanying him in his adventures. The contract also mentions that the pictures were to be accompanied by inscriptions explaining them, and thoroughly researched heraldry, and that it was to be based on a pre-drawn pattern, supplied in the form of a roll. All materials used for the painting were to be of finest quality.

In Florence a bridegroom or his family made house-decoration decisions before the wedding, at which time his house, or a portion of his family's dwelling, usually just a bedroom, was prepared for the young couple. It is sometimes quite noticeable that the bride was unlikely to have been involved in this process, as some bedroom decorations seem to modern eyes rather inappropriate for bedrooms, even misogynistic.

The surviving fourteenth-century wall paintings in one of the well-preserved bedrooms of the Palazzo Davanzati in Florence, which illustrate the thirteenth-century French romance *Chastelaine de Vergi*, belong to this category of decoration. The cycle, painted on one of the top sections of four walls of the room, tells a love story that includes both a narrative of deceit and its consequences. Another equally strange choice of topic for a marital bedroom decoration was Giovanni Boccaccio's story of Nastagio degli Onesti, in which a young woman rejects a marriage proposal and is cruelly punished for it (*Decameron* 5.8). The Florentine Pucci family selected this in 1483 for the wedding of Giannozzo Pucci to Lucrezia Bini and commissioned Botticelli's workshop to illustrate the story across four panels (*spalliere*) for the newly-weds' *camera* in the Palazzo Pucci.

No doubt other tales with similar connotations were occasionally chosen by grooms or their families. Based on writings giving advice on both domestic decoration and family life, sometimes authored by humanists and architects and quite widely circulated, they must have been considered suitable as bedroom decoration. An example of such literature is another work by Alberti, the *Intercenales* ('Dinner Pieces'), a series of short tales written in the 1430s for reading aloud as dinner-time entertainment.

The above examples come from patrician Florentine houses, but decoration of walls with exempla on the occasion of marriage seems also to have been popular in other parts of Europe and in much higher social circles. When Margaret of York, sister of Edward IV and Richard III of England, married Charles the Bold, Duke of Burgundy, in 1468, she found the walls of her apartment in the Bruges Prinsenhof painted with marguerites and hung with tapestries telling the story of chaste Lucretia. On the other hand, the frescoes Botticelli painted in 1480s for the Tornabuoni family at Villa Lemmi depict exempla addressing the groom as well as the bride. The woman seems to be receiving gifts from Venus and the Three Graces and the man is shown in the company of the Seven Liberal Arts.

The popularity of moralising subjects is also evident in other parts of Europe where walls were decorated in the same way. A fourteenth-century English example of such a mural decoration survives in Longthorpe Tower in Northamptonshire. In spite of their relatively frequent occurrence in elite domestic spaces, walls decorated with educative topics are rarely illustrated in miniatures.

WALL HANGINGS AND TAPESTRIES

The most popular tapestries and wall hangings from the late Middle Ages to the Renaissance were decorated with a 'verdure' pattern and produced in many European workshops. More elaborate Renaissance ones could show very naturalistic, three-dimensional jungle-like flora and fauna scenes. Early verdures were two-dimensional and had a characteristic stylised *mille-fleurs* pattern, a design showing clusters of mostly light-coloured flowers on a darker green background representing a meadow. One can see such hangings depicted repeatedly in Italian and Flemish works of art. Manuscript illuminations bear witness to this fashion as well (Fig. 76, 126).

Similar to late medieval verdure in their overall two-dimensional design and aesthetic effect were other stylised floral, or even geometric or heraldic, hangings, which employed various vibrant colours. Lavish sets of these can often be seen in fifteenth-century French illuminations of royal interiors, such as the works of Christine de Pizan or the Bedford Hours (Fig. 8, 9, 45, 56, 131). The Bedford Hours miniatures are especially useful in showing one way that wall textiles were used and displayed by medieval noble families. It may be surprising to modern eyes that the hangings belonging to the Duke of Bedford and his wife in the early fifteenth century obviously did not fit the walls of the interiors they inhabited, as they are shown covering decorative architectural features such as columns, tracery and splendid glazed windows. The reason for this is quite simple

[56]
Anne of Burgundy praying to
her patron saint. The room is
dominated by colourful luxury
fabrics, probably embroidered silk,
displaying the duchess's personal
motto. The duchess is kneeling at
her *prie-dieu*, which is covered with
a throw, reading a devotional book.
The x-framed chair behind her is a
symbolic seat of honour for high-
ranking persons. It is embellished
not only with Anne's motto but
also with her heraldic roundel. A
bulky cushion on the chair adds
both comfort and decoration. The
wall hanging spread in front of
the fully glazed Gothic windows
partially covers them to provide
privacy and splendour. The brick
ceiling is partially painted with
stars on a vibrant blue background.
This was a popular decoration
scheme, particularly for medieval
ecclesiastical vaulted ceilings (e.g.
the Basilica of St Francis in Assisi,
or the Scrovegni or Arena Chapel
in Padua). In the best interiors,
expensive ultramarine pigment
and gold paint were used to create
it. The same materials, ultramarine
and gold, were applied in deluxe
manuscript illuminations. Artists
were often obliged by contract to
use them in commissioned works.

The Bedford Master, Book of Hours (The
Bedford Hours), Paris, *c.* 1423–30; British
Library, Add. MS 18850, fol. 257 v

and universal across Europe. The Middle Ages were nomadic times for noble and royal households: they owned more than one country estate and would travel between them very frequently. Many household items and movable pieces of furniture were often transported together with the family. Large textile wall hangings, being very expensive, and useful as a decoration, insulation or wall partitions, formed a very important part of this baggage and were put up in various interiors during the progress of the court. Like a tent, they recreated a familiar, private space wherever their owners went. French and English courts to some extent continued their medieval tradition of progress from house to house for centuries to come: in the sixteenth century Queen Elizabeth I was still travelling incessantly. However, they also gradually adopted a new fashion of commissioning ensembles of textiles made to measure for particular houses and rooms within them. This change was probably first noticeable in Italy. It was introduced by fifteenth- and sixteenth-century elites who lived in regions where few families had large estates, and their property was scattered over a smaller area than was often the case at this period. As their pattern of life became more settled, they increasingly chose to follow the Renaissance rules for interior architecture and furniture design.

[57]
Peter Comestor writing. The wall and the textile hangings are decorated with a variety of geometric and floral patterns. Note the joined chair with an attached board for writing.

Master of the Bible of Jean de Sy, Guyart des Moulins, *La Bible historiale complétée* (Genesis–Psalms), France, Paris?, 1357; British Library, Royal MS 17 E VII, fol. 2 v

Many costly, rare and sought-after textile hangings came from the Orient. Exotic Turkish or Syrian rugs were not only used as floor coverings but also displayed on walls. Some were thrown over benches or tables. Their depictions in illuminated manuscripts are very rare but a few examples of oriental rugs are well represented in famous miniatures. One of them is a book-presentation scene with portraits of Federico da Montefeltro, Duke of Urbino, and Cristoforo Landino, a Florentine humanist, in his *Disputationes camaldulenses* (MS. Urb. lat. 508, cover verso, now in the Biblioteca Apostolica Vaticana), which is dedicated to the duke. Here an oriental rug is thrown over a window-sill.

While various wall hangings were popular in many affluent households, large-scale figurative and narrative tapestries were luxury items which only the richest elite households could afford. The best collection of these was in the possession of the fifteenth-century Burgundian dukes, which is not surprising, as world-famous tapestries of the highest quality were produced in the Low Countries, especially in Arras, Tournai and Brussels. Indeed, the word 'Arras' is in some languages a synonym for a tapestry. Top-end Flemish tapestries were made of wool enriched by a substantial amount of very expensive silk and gilded metallic thread. Craftsmen producing them were highly skilled and the artistic value and cost of their works surpassed those of paintings.

Tapestries were produced both speculatively and as commissions for individual patrons, who would order them for particular walls or entire rooms. As we know from many surviving fifteenth- and sixteenth-century letters and accounts, the open market often could not provide tapestries that fulfilled the requirements of a discerning client. This forced patrons to commission new tapestries in the Netherlands which were not only made to measure but also executed to a specific design. The practice seems to have been relatively widespread from the mid-fifteenth century. Patrons placing expensive commissions in Netherlandish tapestry workshops were normally members of ruling elites, as only they could afford to finance the manufacture of this type of textile.

Commissions came from all over Europe. In 1515 Pope Leo X (Giovanni di Lorenzo de' Medici) ordered from Raphael a set of cartoons for ten tapestries, which were then woven for him in Brussels between 1516 and 1521. Leo X's tapestries, known as the 'Acts of the Apostles', were usually displayed on important occasions in the Sistine Chapel. One of Raphael's cartoons for them still exists and is displayed in the Victoria and Albert Museum in London. Unfortunately, the tapestries themselves did not survive the 1527 sack of Rome and were probably either burnt or cut into smaller pieces and dispersed. Another set of ten Brussels tapestries using silk and gilt metal threads was commissioned in 1537. Decorated with scenes from the life of the prophet Abraham, it embellished the walls of Henry VIII's Hampton Court Palace. The iconographic purpose of this set was probably to support the role Henry VIII played in the Reformation. The design for the tapestries is attributed to Pieter Coecke van Aelst. Similar Abraham tapestries survive in Vienna and Madrid. Several decades later, between 1550 and 1560, a vast number of tapestries, of which 136 still survive, were produced in the Brussels workshops for Zygmunt II August, King of Poland, who ordered numerous sets for Wawel Castle in Kraków, and his other residences. It was the largest commission for tapestries ever placed by any patron. The tapestries were designed to cover particular walls in rooms and corridors and were hung on undecorated wall surfaces, straight under painted friezes. The surviving historiated cycles of wall paintings by Hans Dürer and Antoni z Wrocławia that cover the upper third of walls in ceremonial rooms in Wawel Castle indicate clearly that the tapestries were suspended directly underneath them and decorated two thirds of the wall surface. Some of the individual pieces of these tapestry cycles measure up to *c.* 5m by 9m. Most of them are decorated with biblical narratives, grotesques, royal personal emblems, heraldic motifs and verdure.

Smaller-scale verdure tapestries, usually made without metallic or silk thread, were produced not only in the Netherlands but also in many other European workshops, which in the later Middle Ages were set mainly along the Rhine and in Switzerland, France and Italy. Even though numerous weavers produced them, some patrons must have preferred to order verdure tapestries from prestigious Netherlandish workshops: in 1482 Filippo Strozzi, a prosperous Florentine banker for whom the Palazzo Strozzi was built, commissioned from Filippino Lippi a design for a verdure tapestry that was intended to serve as a pattern for Netherlandish rather than Italian weavers.

WALL PAINTINGS

Although more affordable than luxurious textile hangings, large-scale murals were an upmarket way of decorating walls, particularly if executed by world-class artists. Even Leonardo da Vinci was engaged in this type of work: in the 1490s, he painted trees and foliage onto the top sections of the walls and the vaulted ceiling of the Sala delle Asse in Castello Sforzesco, the seat of the dukes of Milan, for Ludovico il Moro.

Artists painting murals, like the one decorating a guildhall or some other public building in the illumination from the early sixteenth-century Polish Behem Codex, are very rarely shown in manuscripts (Fig. 58). When they are, it is apparent that illuminators often had great difficulty in executing such depictions convincingly. For instance, the mid-fifteenth-century French 'Talbot Master' in his miniature of Irene, daughter of Cratinus, decorating a church wall in Boccaccio's *Le livre de femmes nobles et renomées*, makes several very obvious composition and perspective mistakes so that the mural overlaps considerably with a part of a glazed window (British Library, Royal MS 16 G V, fol. 73 verso).

Probably chiefly because of the technical difficulty and intricacy involved in depicting large-scale patterned, figurative or historiated wall paintings, which could compromise the clarity of a miniature's composition, representations of such works of art are very infrequent in illuminated manuscripts. They do exist, but it is often difficult or even impossible to tell whether the illumination is showing a mural or a wall hanging. This is because wall paintings often imitated textile or fur hangings, which were more expensive than paintwork. The January illumination from the Très Riches Heures illustrates the problem (Fig. 125). Behind the Duc de Berry's textile canopy, we see a textile hanging, or possibly a mural imitating a hanging. The upper edge of the image showing knights on horseback is alternately raised and sagging at regular intervals, which is a clear indication that the illuminator intended to paint either a textile hanging – probably a tapestry – or a cleverly executed mural mimicking one. This very detailed wall decoration can be compared to another shown in a contemporary French illumination from the *Livre de la Mutation de Fortune* portraying Christine de Pizan admiring a historiated mural in the Salle de Fortune (Bibliothèque Nationale de France, MS Fr. 603, fol. 127 verso). Here we can see a ceiling-to-floor and wall-to-wall block of green background uniformly straight on all edges. One could argue that this illumination must depict a mural, as no attempt is made to indicate a different type of wall ornament. However, the even finishes could be due to the much less detailed nature of this latter miniature, so, frustratingly, one cannot in the end be absolutely sure. Another similarly composed fifteenth-century French illumination of exactly the same scene poses identical questions (Munich, Bayerische Staatsbibliothek, Cod. gall. 11, fol. 53).

(All three illuminations mentioned above show wall decorations containing chivalric scenes, which are frequent in both tapestries and murals. For instance, tournament and jousting contests survive at the fourteenth-century Schloss Runkelstein in Bozen, in

[58]
Miniature from the Kraków Statutes
of the Painters. A painter decorates a
wall with a mural.

Codex picturatus Balthasaris Behem,
Kraków, early 16th century; Biblioteka
Jagiellońska, Kraków, MS 16, fol. 273
(original foliation: 267)

Pisanello's mid-fifteenth-century cycle at the Palazzo Ducale in Mantua, and in an early sixteenth-century cycle of four friezes by Hans Dürer and Antoni z Wrocławia that decorate one of the ceremonial halls at Wawel Castle.)

It is worth exploring the confusing complication caused by the popularity of illusionistic painting, as representations of it in illuminations can easily be misinterpreted. Taking into account the enormous role wall paintings played in high-status interior decoration, this is best done in the context of a short introduction to murals and followed by well-known examples of murals and paintings imitating textiles.

Wall paintings are usually associated with ecclesiastical, mainly church, interiors, but many walls in high-status residences were not only decorated with basic colours or simple ornaments but also embellished with large-scale paintings. Private chapels, such as the one in the Florentine Palazzo Medici, were an obvious location for such decoration. In fact, Benozzo Gozzoli was commissioned to paint the Medici Chapel by Cosimo de' Medici in the late 1450s, soon after the artist, in collaboration with Fra Angelico, had been employed by the same patron to execute devotional frescoes in the otherwise very austere monastic cells of the freshly rebuilt and renovated Dominican convent of San Marco nearby. Just as typically religious murals were suitable for domestic decoration, paintings showing exteriors and interiors of private residences (often complete with a portrait of the patron, who is depicted witnessing events from the lives of the saints) were commissioned for churches. Domenico Ghirlandaio's frescoes in the Santa Fina Chapel at San Gimignano collegiate (1470s) and the Tornabuoni Chapel in Santa Maria Novella in Florence (1480s) are exceptionally good examples of this custom, which was widely practised in late medieval and Renaissance Europe. It would not be too far-fetched to compare this tradition to a similar custom in devotional manuscripts, mainly books of hours, which, although religious in their purpose, use secular domestic imagery not only in calendar pages but also, typically, in portraits of evangelists and in Annunciation and Nativity scenes. Many other events such as Pentecost or, more rarely, Christ before Annas were treated in a similar way.

The murals mentioned above, which are well preserved and documented, date from the fifteenth century, but wall paintings adorned European churches, monasteries and noble and middle-class homes long before then. Medieval secular wall paintings very rarely survive, owing to frequent redecoration, remodelling of room layouts or deterioration. The survival rate of wall paintings often depends on the technique used to execute them. A large proportion of well-preserved medieval and Renaissance murals are found in Italy for this very reason. Italian artists often employed the standard and very robust *buon fresco* (true fresco) technique of painting with pigments on wet plaster. True fresco was also known and used elsewhere, but northern European painters especially were frequently tempted to experiment with wall decoration on dry plaster. This allowed them painting with oils, glazing, gilding and application of gemstones, which enhanced the sumptuous effect but made the murals less durable.

Famous surviving fourteenth-century examples of murals include those in Schloss Runkelstein in Bozen, the Palazzo del Podestà in San Gimignano and the Palazzo Davanzati in Florence. They all use fashionable motifs: architectural ornaments, landscapes, coats of arms, floral or geometric patterns, biblical or classical subjects and courtly narratives and pastimes, such as jousting, hunting, dancing or games. Paintings of this kind were most suitable for halls or even bedrooms.

Some domestic wall paintings, like two in the Palazzo del Podestà showing a young couple bathing together and, subsequently, in their bed, are private in nature and possibly once decorated bedrooms where they were intended, maybe clumsily to modern eyes, to encourage couples to procreate, which was their family and civic duty. One of the much more sophisticated masterpieces of secular interior decoration, portions of which take love imagery a step further, is an allegorical, zodiacal fresco cycle in the Salone dei Mesi in the Palazzo Schifanoia. The charming wall paintings of this Ferrarese pleasure palace belonging to the d'Este family were executed primarily by Francesco del Cossa and Cosme Tura between 1476 and 1484. Later wall paintings, mannerist in style and visually stunning, found at a Gonzaga pleasure palace near Mantua, the Palazzo del Te, are a pinnacle of frivolous interior decoration. This truly extravagant palladian villa, together with its decorative scheme referencing mainly classical subjects, was designed by Giulio Romano, an architect and painter, for Federico II Gonzaga in the first half of the sixteenth century.

TEXTILE WALL HANGINGS IMITATED IN MURALS AND PAINTINGS

At about the same time as the Palazzo Schifanoia frescoes, another masterpiece, different in tone, came into existence when Mantegna was commissioned by Ludovico Gonzaga to decorate the Camera degli Sposi at the Palazzo Ducale on the occasion of his wedding to Barbara of Brandenburg. This work, started in 1465 and finalised nine years later in 1474, is full of dignity and gravitas, stressing the Gonzagas' elevated place in society. The elaborate decoration on the walls and the ceiling, alive with masterly *trompe l'oeil* effects, employed purely Renaissance ornaments that provided an elegant setting to classical narratives, large-scale landscapes and, above all, spectacular group portraits of the Gonzaga family, their allies and courtiers. Extremely expensive Netherlandish tapestries, made to order, would normally have been a fitting decoration for rooms of this class. However, Mantegna's paintings cover the entire wall surfaces, not leaving any space for other types of wall embellishment. Instead, abundant luxurious textiles are rendered as illusions in the frescoes.

A similar device had been used by earlier painters and decorators. Fourteenth-century frescoes in a Florentine merchant house, the Palazzo Davanzati, are full of realistically rendered textile hangings, which appear to be suspended by metal rings from hooks and curled up at their edges above the floor, revealing non-illusionistic, standard medieval wall decoration underneath and, in one case, a historiated *Chastelaine de Vergi* fresco cycle painted under the ceiling of one of the bedrooms.

Other northern European fourteenth-century murals from ecclesiastical and domestic settings also contain figurative historiated scenes accompanied by paintings imitating textile hangings. A famous surviving example of this is to be seen in murals in the Ehingenhof in Ulm, where the wall is divided into two main zones. The upper one is decorated with two figures, one female and one male, surrounded by an abstract floral pattern and inscriptions. In the lower zone, beneath the couple's feet, is a painting of a textile suspended from a dado.

Another spectacular and well-preserved fourteenth-century mural cycle with textile imitations can still be seen in the *chambre du cerf* of the Papal Palace in Avignon. Here also the wall is divided into horizontal zones. The main central strip of the wall is devoted to methods of hunting and fishing, shown against a lush green backdrop of trees and meadows. The zone below is painted with traditional textile wall hangings. Given the similarity of style and subjects, it is very likely that the Avignon murals inspired some of the (also surviving) interior wall decoration of the Casa Datini in Prato, a house built for Francesco Datini, a fabulously wealthy Tuscan merchant who spent several decades – and made his fortune – in Avignon in the late fourteenth and early fifteenth centuries.

Depictions of textiles are also quite frequent in panel paintings and illuminations. It is no coincidence that both northern and southern European artistic centres, such as Bruges and Florence, thrived not only on banking and trade but also on the cloth industry, as textiles – especially silk, cloth of gold and tapestries – were a luxury. Artists in cities importing and producing expensive fabrics would certainly have had access to a choice of samples. These were kept, or more probably copied, and served as workshop models. Many figures on paintings are shown not only against a backdrop of luxurious wall hangings, sometimes even generously flowing onto the floor, but also seated on cushions and dressed in equally splendid materials. Since many fabrics, especially silks imported from the Orient, were extremely expensive and became decorative status symbols, depicting them in all types of media was very popular and stayed in fashion across Europe for centuries. Some painters' workshops, such as the fourteenth-century Florentine di Cione brothers' workshop (Orcagna and his brothers), seem to have specialised in devotional images of this kind. As testified by contemporary orders placed by art dealers who sold them at the papal seat in Avignon, pictures depicting rich fabrics must have been sought after by many. Paintings of this kind were affordable to the lower nobility or the middle classes, who would not have been able to buy the textiles depicted on them, and were purchased by pilgrims. These souvenirs, taken home by the pilgrims, could serve as house altar and attractive wall decoration in one. Contemporary representations of interiors in panel paintings, woodcuts and illuminations show devotional images on walls of bedrooms, studies and halls. Unfortunately, the scale of devotional paintings depicted in paintings and miniatures is usually far too tiny to tell whether the originals portrayed

[59]
Boethius in his library. The very
large, secular picture hanging on its
own on the wall is not a frequent
feature in fifteenth-century interiors.

Attributed to Jean Colombe, Boethius, *Le
Livre de Boece de Consolacion* (anonymous
French translation), Book 1, Bourges, 1477;
British Library, Harley MS 4335, fol. 1

luxurious fabrics. Also, they are frequently completely or partially covered by curtains
or tabernacle doors. Several fifteenth- and sixteenth-century Flemish and French miniatures of Annunciation and Pentecost scenes depict examples of partially or completely
covered devotional pictures and religious sculptures. Placed against walls, or attached to
them, they stand directly on buffets on which candles could be arranged to illuminate the
works of art when revealed for prayer or meditation (Fig. 11).

PAINTINGS

Free-hanging, independent, large-scale, framed and uncovered easel paintings were
known in the Middle Ages, but did not become commonly used as a standard and
frequent wall ornament in private houses until the Renaissance. Such paintings were
rarely depicted in manuscripts and the late fifteenth-century Flemish illumination
showing Boethius in a library decorated with a very sizeable secular painting suspended
by means of a chain and hook on an otherwise bare wall is one of few exceptions (Fig.
59). Inventories give a fair amount of helpful information on types of paintings, including
painted furniture, and on their distribution in the house. It is worth noting that pictures

(at least those not integrated into chests) were often displayed above head-height. In Flanders and Italy they were sometimes placed above doors or on tall pieces of furniture or attached to the wall above them. For instance, as already mentioned, according to one of the Medici inventories, Botticelli's *Primavera* was displayed in a bedroom above a *lettuccio*, a piece of furniture that usually had a rather high backrest. Two Florentine editions of Savonarola's *Predica del arte del ben morire* (one printed in 1496–7 and another in *c.* 1500) with woodcut depictions of devotional paintings confirm this fashion. There, a *tondo* in the earlier and a tabernacle in the later edition are fixed to the walls above head-height and next to *lettucci* cornices.

Most medieval and Renaissance independent paintings (that is, not integrated into or associated with furniture pieces or wall decoration) in private interiors were small in size and often covered with a curtain or doors. An exceptionally good example of a devotional picture with attached doors can be seen in George Trubert's illusionistic miniature of the Virgin in the Chester Beatty Book of Hours (Malibu, J. Paul Getty Museum, MS. 48, fol. 159). Another illumination, by Simon Bening in the Prayer Book of Cardinal Albrecht of Brandenburg, shows how a devotional picture (also with doors) was displayed in Flanders in the early sixteenth century. The painting is placed against a wall and above a very tall Gothic buffet, next to the entrance door of a hall (Malibu, J. Paul Getty Museum, MS. Ludwig IX 19, fol. 87 verso). Another contemporary Flemish illumination by the Master of the David Scenes in the Grimani Breviary shows a devotional statue surrounded by curtains also placed on a buffet and in a very similar setting (Fig. 10). The same artist depicts a buffet with drawn curtains above it in the Virgin Mary's bedroom; one can only assume that a religious image is hidden behind them (Fig. 11).

Paintings were usually executed in tempera or oil, on a panel or canvas. Some very small ones were made by book illuminators on parchment. These could also have been painted by artists working as both illuminators and panel painters. In fact many manuscript illuminations do look like independent paintings and are surrounded by an illusionistic picture frame (Fig. 10, 25, 47, 60, 75, 87, 111, 130). University of Oxford, Bodleian Library, MS Douce 112 – from which many examples in this book are drawn – has on fol. 16 verso a framed, full-page Virgin and Child miniature that fulfils all the criteria of a small religious painting for hanging on a wall or placing on top of a piece of furniture against a wall. Some miniatures of this kind were produced and sold on loose leaves. They could either be incorporated into a manuscript illuminated by other artists, or used as a detached devotional painting. The subject of paintings made for private use was mostly religious. The Virgin and Child seem to have been a universal favourite, especially for bedrooms (Fig. 61, 137). Fourteenth- and fifteenth-century artists based in Florence and Bruges produced many of these, some made on commission and some for the open market. A number of such paintings, some by artists such as Memling and Botticelli, still survive.

The circular *tondo* was popular in Italy and Flanders in the fifteenth century but most pictures were rectangular. Some of these had arched tops. Now often detached, rectangular panels may have belonged to diptychs or triptychs. Larger polyptychs were often commissioned for churches as altarpieces. In the case of multipart paintings, the religious image would normally be accompanied by portraits of the donors, often paired up with their patron saints. Good examples of these are Flemish Annunciations mentioned earlier, and other panel paintings produced in Bruges, such as Memling's diptych of Maarten Nieuwenhove. In this exquisite composition St Martin appears as a stained glass window insert. Memling's portraits of the Florentine Tommaso Portinari and his wife possibly also flanked a devotional image (*c.* 1470, Metropolitan Museum of Art).

Flemish artists, especially van Eyck and Memling, and their works had a groundbreaking influence on the development of naturalistic portraiture in Italy and elsewhere. Many such pictures, made predominantly for private use, by artists in Bruges and Florence were commissioned on the occasion of a marriage, but some commemorate dead family members, such as the portrait of Giovanna degli Albizzi Tornabuoni by Domenico Ghirlandaio (1488, Museo Thyssen-Bornemisza, Madrid) and that of Giuliano de' Medici by Botticelli (1476–8, three versions, now in Bergamo, Berlin and Washington).

Portraits of individuals could also be produced on parchment. At first such portraits were incorporated into manuscripts. Author portraits, very idealised, go back to the early Middle Ages and depict evangelists or scribe monks (Fig. 2). Later medieval and Renaissance patron portraits appear mainly in presentation scenes (Fig. 8, 62). From the sixteenth century onwards portrait miniatures produced as independent works of art became fashionable, such as Simon Bening's self-portraits of 1558 (now in the Victoria and Albert Museum and the Metropolitan Museum of Art).

Another type of commemorative painting for family use is a birth-tray (*desco da parto*). Typically Tuscan, they were presented to young mothers after the arrival of children. Originally they were probably plain trays used to serve a nourishing meal to the young mother after the birth. This custom is depicted in many illuminations. In the fifteenth century they were fashionably decorated with historiated symbolic or allegorical scenes, personal insignia and coats of arms. Families usually kept them as bedroom ornaments and may have displayed them on the walls. One such high-status tray was commissioned on the occasion of Lorenzo de' Medici's birth and painted by Scheggia *c.* 1449 (now at the Metropolitan Museum of Art , New York).

Finally, decorative subjects popular in other artistic media, such as battles, jousts and scenes from vernacular or classic literature and history, were also represented on paintings. Many still exist and are displayed as detached pictures, though one has to bear in mind that it is now difficult to tell (without detailed examination and scientific research) which of them are deprived of their original context and were previously parts of a larger wall panelling or panels integrated into or produced *en suite* with furniture like chests, beds or daybeds. Sections of such historiated wall panelling, which subsequently may have been cut down and framed as separate smaller paintings, can be seen on the illumination to the Sforza Hours (Fig. 60). The illumination border moreover employs a very convincing *trompe l'oeil* effect and imitates exactly the design of frames around the wall panelling, which, as we saw above, makes the miniature look like a framed panel painting of the Last Supper.

3. Ceilings

OPEN TIMBER ROOF AND BEAMED CEILINGS

Most European ceilings had exposed beams. Northern European medieval timber barns and farmhouses had no ceiling or attic floor, so that the complicated timber structure supporting the roof was exposed. Depending on the status of the building, the beams, consisting of vertical posts, horizontal purlins, sloping rafters, braces, trusses and so on, were either plain or richly carved and painted. Open timber roofs could be very striking and were often the principal decorative feature in the great halls of English and Scottish medieval castles and manor houses. Alas, illuminations seldom show

[62]
Presentation scene. Jean de Meun presenting his translation of Boethius to King Philip IV. This royal interior does not have much furniture but its walls are fully covered with costly textile hangings decorated with the fleur-de-lis, a French royal device.

Attributed to Jean Colombe, Boethius, *Le Livre de Boece de consolacion* (anonymous French translation), Book 1, Bourges, 1477; British Library, Harley MS 4335, fol. 10

[63]
The Annunciation scene in the Virgin Mary's bedroom. The walls and the beamed timber ceiling are undecorated apart from the carved beam end. The furniture is Gothic in style.

Attributed to the Master of the Flemish Boethius, Jean Aubert, *La vie de notre seigneur Jhesucrist, La Vengance de la mort Jhesu Christ*, Ghent, 1479; British Library, Royal MS 16 G III, fol. 18 v

structures opened to the roof and a depiction in a peasants' house interior in the Très Riches Heures is a rare example (Fig. 53).

Flat beamed ceilings, on the other hand, are a recurring motif in European manuscripts, as the majority of European domestic buildings were fitted with them (Fig. 1, 37, 48, 58, 62, 63, 72, 77, 86, 103). This most popular type of ceiling consisted of main beams, or timber joists, spanning the width of the room. They rested on horizontal, decorative corbels and supported two layers of smaller beams arranged at right angles. The beams and the rectangular spaces between them were often carved and decorated with painted ornaments: geometric designs, heraldry, flora, fauna and portraits were the most frequent motifs.

Vaulted timber ceilings were very popular in northern Europe, especially in France and Flanders, and are depicted in numerous illuminations produced in those countries. A few such ceilings still survive, such as the imposing *charpente lambrisée* vault at the Hôtel-Dieu Notre-Dame in Tonnerre, Burgundy. Such boarded vaulted ceilings, with decorative tiebeams and king struts that were also part of the roof structure, were typical in late medieval France (Fig. 8).

Although not represented in illuminations, some very impressive medieval open timber roofs still exist. The most famous examples in the United Kingdom can be admired in Westminster Hall in London and in the Great Hall of Stirling Castle.

Flat beamed and vaulted ceilings are well documented in pictorial sources, especially in fifteenth-century Flemish illuminations, and have survived in numerous extant buildings, many of which are in Bruges. A good example of a decorated fifteenth-century beamed ceiling can be seen just round the corner from the Bruges illuminators' quarter in Hof van Bladelin. Other fifteenth-century beamed ceilings are known from the most prestigious Bruges residences: Prinsenhof, Hof van Gruuthuse, Hof van Watervliet and Hof van Adornes. Corbels and beams of such ceilings were usually decorated with family coats of arms, personal emblems and the mottos of the owners and of the princes with whom the owners were allied.

VAULTED STONE AND BRICK CEILINGS

Vaulted stone or brick ceilings were normally installed in churches and in cellars and on the ground floors of domestic or institutional buildings, throughout the Middle Ages and the Renaissance (Fig. 9, 35, 56, 64, 66, 87, 94). Thousands of them survive across Europe. In private, and in particular in merchant houses, sturdy, well-insulated and secure vaulted cellars were commonly used as storage areas for wine, perishable foods and valuable goods. One of the fourteenth-century illuminations shows such a timber vaulted room serving as a wine cellar. Other depictions from the same manuscript, Cocharelli's *Treatise on the Vices*, show (or indicate with columns) vaulted rooms as bankers' (or pawnbrokers') offices (Fig. 54, 108).

Aesthetically very appealing, vaulted ceilings were a highly desirable feature for formal rooms. However, these were customarily on the upper floors of buildings, which often could not support very heavy masonry, and had 'fake' vaulted ceilings made of timber and sometimes finished with plaster and stucco (Fig. 10, 43, 61, 65, 112, 118).

Vaulted ceilings in formal rooms or in private domestic chapels are represented in countless illuminations from all over Europe. These usually do not indicate clearly the material from which vaults were built, but one can get a very good idea about the type of design and the colour schemes used for their decoration. The favourite colour seems to have been blue. In symbolic imitation of a sky at night, blue vaults – especially those in chapels, but also in private interiors – were frequently painted with stylised gold stars, often placed at regular intervals, creating a theatrical effect of a ceiling opening up to the sky and to God (Fig. 9, 64, 66, 94). Renaissance ceilings could also be decorated with coffering, which often used the same blue and gold palette and similar ornamental motifs, though medieval stars often evolved into rosettes and other designs (British Library, Yates Thompson MS 30, fol. 30 verso). Many Renaissance vaulted ceilings were frescoed, often including walls, with historiated or *trompe l'oeil* effect designs. One such ingenious fresco by Leonardo da Vinci can be seen in the Sala delle Asse in Castello Sforzesco.

PANELLED AND COFFERED CEILINGS

Panelled ceilings were much more exclusive and high status than beamed ceilings, and were typical during the Renaissance. Such ceilings were suspended flat structures attached to the joists of beamed ceilings. They consisted of thin wooden panels, which at first created rectangular, often square, flat sections, all of equal size. These could have mouldings surrounding them and creating a coffering effect. The mouldings and coffers were often carved, polychromed and gilded. As in other types of ceilings, blue was still a popular colour for coffers. They were also frequently decorated with gilded rosettes and bosses – maybe a modified variation on the stars seen on earlier vaulted ceilings. From the beginning of the sixteenth century coffers became deeper, irregularly sized and shaped, adopting classical schemes. Illuminations usually show panelled or coffered ceilings in very affluent Renaissance settings. These can range from well-equipped patrician studies to royal palace interiors (Fig. 33, 47, 66, 100, 111, 137).

Panelled and especially coffered ceilings are well represented in Flemish and Italian illuminations. As they developed in Italy, one of the most beautiful, famous and interesting Renaissance coffered ceilings is also Italian. It was commissioned for the Sala dei Gigli (Hall of Lilies), a Florentine government meeting room in the Palazzo della Signoria (now the Palazzo Vecchio) and designed and executed in the 1470s by Giuliano and Benedetto da Maiano and painted in the 1480s by other artists. The ceiling consists of deep hexagonal coffers painted blue and decorated with gilded rosettes and radiating fleur-de-lis. Three of the walls of the Sala dei Gigli echo the design of the ceiling. The fourth is frescoed by Domenico Ghirlandaio. The decoration of this seemingly unpretentious ceiling makes a very strong political statement. The fleur-de-lis, an emblem of Florence to this day, was first and foremost a French royal device (mainly and very

[64]
St Mark in his study. The ceiling is vaulted and decorated with gold stars on a blue ground, imitating the sky at night.

Book of Hours, France (Amiens), between 1430 and 1440; British Library, Add. MS 31835, fol. 18 v

[65]
Pentecost in an opulent Flemish interior. The vaulted ceiling and carved buffet are painted with bright colours. A maiolica vase, a candlestick and a wine jug stand on the buffet in front of a covered devotional painting (apparently a diptych, possibly of an Annunciation scene?). Note the sconce above the door with its shiny metal disc reflecting the light.

Attributed to the workshop of the Master of James IV of Scotland, Book of Hours (Hours of Joanna I of Castile), Flemish (Ghent?), c. 1500; British Library, Add. MS 35313, fol. 33 v

[66]
St Matthew in his study. The interior has a coffered cross-vaulted ceiling decorated with stars.

Muzio Attendolo Master, Book of Hours (Hours of Bona Sforza), Milan, c. 1490–4; British Library, Add. MS 34294, fol. 7

extensively applied in French royal settings, as shown in numerous illuminations; Fig. 8, 62). Following the French victory over the Ghibellines at Benevento in 1266, which made Florence independent of the empire, a Florentine lily was traditionally associated with the protection of its republican liberty by the French kings. This republican symbol gained an additional heraldic dynastic connotation in Florentine culture in 1465, when King Louis XI of France gave Piero de' Medici and his descendants the right to add three gold fleur-de-lis on a blue ground to their coat of arms. Piero's son, Lorenzo the Magnificent, is known to have used this device on several occasions. Commissioned and completed during Lorenzo de' Medici's de facto rule of Florence, the design of the ceiling and of the rest of the decoration of the Sala dei Gigli was controlled by Lorenzo's artistic taste and political ideology. In this context, the fleur-de-lis device can be seen as an assertion of Lorenzo's power and becomes an ambiguous symbol merging Florentine republican liberty with Medicean dynastic ambitions. Maybe unsurprisingly, about a century later, the Medici family made the Palazzo della Signoria their private residence when they became hereditary Grand Dukes of Tuscany and the republic ceased to exist.

The idea of employing the fleur-de-lis emblem to carry a political alliance and ennoblement message was not a new one in Tuscany. In 1391 two Florentine painters, Bartolomeo di Bertozzo and Agnolo di Taddeo Gaddi, were commissioned by Francesco di Marco Datini, a spectacularly wealthy new-moneyed merchant keen to proclaim his association with French royalty, to decorate the vaulted ceiling on the ground floor of his new house in Prato with yellow lilies on a blue ground. Datini's house and large parts of its original decoration scheme still survive and are very interesting specimens of architecture and interior decoration. In addition to these, his well-preserved, very extensive business archive and private correspondence are exceptionally rich tools for the study of late fourteenth- and early fifteenth-century social, cultural and economic contexts.

Renaissance architects put much effort into ceiling design. Sebastiano Serlio, in his *Regole generali di architettura* (Venice, 1537), published numerous plates with designs for coffered ceilings. Many of these were scrupulously replicated in high-status European houses. Henry VIII's building projects were no exception. For instance, the ceiling of the so-called Wolsey Closet in Hampton Court Palace was evidently based on one of Serlio's designs. It must have been executed shortly after 1537, the year of publication of Serlio's book and of Edward VI's birth. Decorated with Prince of Wales feathers, the ceiling was modified for Henry VIII's objective: a celebration of the arrival of the long-awaited male heir to the English throne and assertion of his legitimacy. Like that of the Sala dei Gigli, the Hampton Court ceiling is not only an ornamental piece of interior decoration; it also carries a political message and becomes a device clearly affirming Tudor dynastic continuity.

Not all high-status coffered ceilings were necessarily tools of propaganda. Those executed in a stable political climate were more likely to be playful and did not have to communicate ambitious agendas. To this category belongs another surviving coffered ceiling, in the Sala Poselska (Envoys' Hall) in Wawel Castle in Kraków. It consists of very deep, richly carved, polychromed and gilded rectangular coffers, the mouldings of which served as frames for 194 sculpted heads – portraits of kings, courtiers, nobility, patricians, literary figures and many others. The ceiling was commissioned in 1535 by Zygmunt I from Sebastian Tauerbach, and thirty of the original portraits still exist in situ.

A contemporary coffered ceiling also showing portraits, though inspired by and filled mainly with antique motifs, was fitted at James V's Stirling Castle in Scotland, the seat of the Stewart dynasty. The ceiling, dated to *c.* 1540–2, was probably executed by Scottish and French artisans. It has been dismantled but many of the portraits still survive.

V

ESSENTIAL COMFORTS, MATERIAL POSSESSIONS AND THEIR DISTRIBUTION IN DOMESTIC SPACE

In the Middle Ages many European houses, both in towns and in the countryside, had one main room, a hall, which was a living space serving multiple functions and used by the whole family, guests and servants. All daily activities took place there and at night the room was turned into a temporary bedroom for all the inhabitants (Fig. 4). The tendency to separate private space from the hall was first visible in affluent, large houses. In such dwellings, often the most important person in the household would have their own room. Such rooms were private, access to them was restricted and beds often became their permanent fixture although, like halls, they were still used by their owners for many purposes (Fig. 5–8, 67).

Houses with specialised rooms having one function developed gradually and became widespread in Europe by about the mid-sixteenth century, when new types of single-use rooms came into being, such as dining room or gallery. Royalty and the comfort of royal residences led the way, and were imitated by other classes. As mentioned before, this trend, which originated in the late Middle Ages and developed fully in the Renaissance, was accelerated and driven by complex cultural, political, social and economic changes, such as Italian humanist thought and its art and architecture applied in the domestic sphere, the growing wealth of the merchant and banker classes, the increased importance of towns, and the decline of feudalism, which led to a change of lifestyle for royalty and the nobility from peripatetic to settled. Medieval feudal lords, once overseeing vast territories, became sophisticated Renaissance courtiers. They no longer needed to build and maintain castles that were secure against enemy attack, and instead used their wealth to develop well-designed and well-furnished comfortable town and country residences. The middle classes, especially merchants and bankers of considerable financial means and political ambition, not only imitated royalty and nobles but, in the case of Florentine patricians, became precursors of new Renaissance trends and lifestyles. Not coincidentally this development was reinforced, associated and connected with visible changes in architecture, furnishings and domestic material culture (see pp. 13–14).

Not much furniture survives that can be dated before 1300. From that time, there are also few written sources mentioning furniture. Although illustrations (most of them in

[67]
A man warming his hands by a fire either in a hall or in a private room. The fireplace contains a pot crane and an andiron. The window is fully glazed. The room has two panelled benches with backs, a barrelled seat and a round dining table. The assemblage is similar to those in other illuminations of meals being served, apparently in parlours or chambers, but no bed is visible in this miniature.

Petrus de Crescentiis, *Rustican des ruraulx prouffiz du labour des champs* (*Ruralia commoda*, trans. into French attributed to Jean Corbechon), Bruges, last quarter of the 15th century *c.* 1478–*c.* 1480; British Library, Royal MS 14 E VI, fol. 305 v illuminated manuscripts) showing early furniture do exist, their potential is limited as, in the absence of other types of evidence supporting their reliability as realistic representations, they are not dependable. However, from the late 1300s and early 1400s, there is a notable increase in surviving furniture types. Moreover, the quantity and quality both of paintings and illuminations showing furniture pieces (not overly stylised, and looking realistic) and of written documentation (accounts, wills, inventories, travel journals) available provide dependable context and verification for one another. This change was associated with a multitude of socio-economic and cultural factors, among which technical developments in furniture production and the transformation of lifestyle, resulting in greater appreciation of domestic comfort, were crucial.

Heating and a water supply were essential for comfortable domestic life and their history is closely connected to and inseparable from the development of kitchens and bathrooms. Artificial lighting predominantly depended on the open fire used for heating, although many other forms of light source were also available to those who could afford them. Water supply, vital for survival, cooking and hygiene, was always a major concern. Primitive settlements depended on water from rivers and streams but the construction of wells, cisterns and aqueducts had already been developed in Antiquity. Some classical technical knowledge was lost after the decline of the Roman Empire, but running hot and cold water, from taps, and plumbing were available in elite European dwellings – mainly royal, princely or monastic – not only in the Renaissance but also in the Middle Ages.

1. Heating and Kitchens

HYPOCAUSTS AND OPEN HEARTHS

Open hearths were the primary heating source employed in most houses in the Middle Ages. This may be surprising, as the ancient Romans had had extremely sophisticated heating systems at their disposal. The best were the hypocausts, which were mainly installed in villas and public baths. They distributed hot air through the floors and walls of buildings by means of channels run in the stone or brick walls and were able to keep the interiors at constant and pleasant temperature and humidity levels. However, they vanished in the early Middle Ages, together with the associated technical know-how needed to build and maintain them. Maybe hypocausts simply did not seem practical and economically viable when many early medieval houses, especially in the northern parts of Europe, were built not of stone or brick but, owing to local tradition and the natural resources available, of timber. Although underfloor heating was re-introduced in Renaissance Italy (for instance in sixteenth-century Padua, as confirmed by extant remains and contemporary drawings), hypocausts were costly to build and maintain and they did not regain the popularity they had enjoyed in Antiquity. Instead, open hearths were used throughout Europe, from castles to peasants' dwellings. In England they were popular much longer than in the rest of Europe. As a fire precaution, they were normally positioned away from walls in the middle of a room and had a stone or brick base (these are known from written sources and archaeological evidence but unfortunately are rarely depicted in illuminations). They were used both for heating and for cooking. Supports for cauldrons and for roasting spits were arranged over or next to them. The smoke from such a hearth escaped through the windows, doors and roof (Fig. 68). Although this must have been quite a nuisance at times, the lack of a chimney was useful for food preservation purposes, as many products, mainly cuts of meat, were hung under the roof over the hearth and were cured and dried in the smoke, which helped conserve them and added flavour. The same practice was continued when fireplaces became common. It can be seen in the January calendar page of a Flemish Psalter, now in the Bodleian Library (Fig. 4), which shows a feasting scene in the third quarter of the thirteenth century.

[68]
Calendar page for January. A cottage with a peasant interior.

Attributed to the young Simon Bening, texts and decoration added to a Book of Hours, Bruges, *c.* 1510–*c.* 1515; British Library, Egerton MS 1147, fol. 6 v

[69]
Calendar page for February.
Warming by a fire.

Book of Hours, France (Amiens), between
1430 and 1440; British Library, Add. MS
31835, fol. 2 v

Exactly the same way of preserving meat products is depicted in a German 1250s calendar page for the month of February (Würzburger Psalter, Bayerische Staatsbibliothek, Munich). The composition of the illumination is very similar to the Bodleian Library's Flemish January scene. It is also supposed to be the earliest known image of a wood-burning tiled stove.

FIREPLACES

Of all sources of heat, the most popular, though not the most effective or efficient, were fireplaces. Very impressive and often ornate and flamboyant components of many interiors, fireplaces with their chimneypieces were recurrently depicted in contemporary illuminations, drawings, woodcuts, etchings and paintings (Fig. 5–7, 10, 13, 36, 37, 67, 69–76, 80, 81, 97, 125, 126).

Fireplaces were described in numerous contemporary journals and letters. Both their merits and the theory of their design were discussed and presented in detail in writings by the best architects, such as Alberti, Serlio, Filarete, Giulio Romano and Antonio da Sangallo. Many medieval and Renaissance fireplaces survive either in situ or in museums and private collections. Their decorative surrounds and remains of anthropomorphic corbels seem to have been especially sought after as collectors' items or were re-used in modern fireplaces.

Although held in high esteem, Italian fireplaces, especially Renaissance ones, were often concealed by fitting them into the overall, sometimes ostentatious decoration scheme of a room. And while they do feature in Italian art, Flemish art seems to have given its local fireplaces much more prominence. This must have reflected a difference in

[70]
Calendar page for February. Feasting
and dancing in a hall. The opulent
fireplace dominates the interior. See
also page 2.

Simon Bening and workshop, Book of
Hours (Golf Book), Bruges, probably early
1540s; British Library, Add. MS 24098,
fol. 19 v

contemporary aesthetical preferences in these two distant parts of Europe. Flemish panel paintings of domestic interiors proudly show a whole range of architectural elements, furniture and objects, but it seems that fireplaces and windows were the main architectural focal point. Similar importance was given to benches habitually placed in front of them, and to fireplace equipment. Flemish fireplaces were imposing not only because of the vast amount of space they took up in a room but also because of their monumental beauty. These characteristics were often exploited by sovereigns, who had their seats placed directly before the fireplace so that they appeared to be framed by an elegant chimneypiece. These, suitably 'dressed' with costly hangings draped around them and fixed to the hoods of fireplaces, transformed the whole ensemble into a throne fit for a noble, a duke, a prince or even a king. Such thrones can be seen on countless Flemish and French illuminations depicting a member of the aristocracy, or occasionally of the upper middle classes, presiding over a private or official gathering such as a festivity, a reception or a court session (Fig. 70, 71, 125, 126).

In spite of all the splendour associated with them, fireplaces had a humble beginning. In their early days they were not much more than open hearths placed against a wall. Combined with a hood and a chimney, they were a technical innovation. In theory, this construction prevented smoke from filling the room as it was caught by the hood above the hearth and was directed straight into the chimney. Reality appears to have been different: as late as the sixteenth century Flemish illuminations show peasant dwellings with waves of smoke escaping through windows and doors, even if a chimney is visible on the roof. However, when fireplaces are depicted in peasant dwellings, details of their construction or decoration are rarely shown, even in the very best illuminations,

[71]
Calendar page for January. Jean, Comte de Dunois, feasting. The wall hanging and chimneypiece bear his personal heraldry. The composition of this miniature is based on the January scene in the Très Riches Heures du Duc de Berry.

The Dunois Master (associate of the Bedford Master), Book of Hours (The Dunois Hours), Paris, c. 1440–c. 1450 (after 1436); British Library, Yates Thompson MS 3, fol. 1

[72]
The Holy Family in a Netherlandish artisan interior. The Virgin Mary, St Joseph and the baby Jesus are sitting by the fire in a poor artisan interior, probably a kitchen/ sitting room. Note the conical fireplace hood. The wall cupboard and shelves are filled with simple wooden, ceramic and metal kitchen utensils and tableware.

The Hours of Catherine of Cleves, Utrecht, 1440; Morgan Library and Museum, New York, MS M. 917, p. 151

such as those from the Très Riches Heures of the Duc de Berry and the Golf Book (Fig. 12, 53).

To catch smoke, early fireplaces had very large conical hoods. To save space, they were placed either in the corner of the room or against its narrowest wall. They were common in the fourteenth century and some of the spectacular fourteenth-century examples of conical hooded fireplaces occupying room corners still survive, for instance in the Palazzo Davanzati in Florence. A rare depiction of a conical fireplace hood can be seen in an illumination from the famous Hours of Catherine of Cleves, produced in Utrecht *c.* 1440 and now in the Morgan Library and Museum in New York (Fig. 72). It shows Mary and Joseph with the infant Jesus in a humble and run-down but charming kitchen/dining room. The holy family are warming themselves at the fireplace and a simple meal is being cooked in a cauldron hung over the hearth. The illumination is exceptional as it shows in detail the modest but comfortable interior of an artisan's family home. Not coincidentally, an associated illumination in the same manuscript shows another room, a workshop, which looks as if it belonged to the same household and was used by Joseph for carpentry, by Mary for weaving, and by the young Jesus as a playground. The workshop also has a fireplace, though it is of a more modern type and has a wedge-shaped hood. Indeed, most later fireplace hoods were wedge-shaped and, although these were very popular in fifteenth-century Italy and France, they feature mostly in Flemish illuminations (Fig. 10, 36, 37, 73, 81, 114). Canopied fireplace hoods were also very popular in Flanders (Fig. 70, 126).

[73]
Calendar page for December. A man warming himself by the fireplace. Note the wedge-shaped hood. The chair is typically Italian.

Style of Giovanni Boccardi; Breviary, Use of Vallombrosa, Florence, last quarter of the 15th century; British Library, Egerton MS 2973, fol. 8 v

Originally hoods were plain, especially in modest homes. As on stove tiles, coats of arms, personal emblems and other family insignia were a popular decoration among the nobility and the upper middle classes. On fireplaces, they were normally inserted in the middle of the hood or chimneypiece. As fireplaces were the main source of light after sunset and in the winter, and they had a fireproof, mostly brick, outer hearth (Fig. 50), their chimneypieces, especially in Flanders, were used for attaching sconces for candles to provide additional light (Fig. 74, 75). Sconces themselves were also a decoration of unadorned chimneypieces, although as the fifteenth century progressed, hoods became increasingly ornamental and could be lavishly decorated with religious or secular sculptures and reliefs (Fig. 10, 74, 126).

Fireplace hoods were supported by side walls, brackets or columns. These were frequently very ornamental and their development reflected general changes in architectural styles. For instance, a French fireplace hood in the Berry book of hours is held up by side walls and columns with foliate capitals, similar to those supporting vaulted

[74]
'Hommes sauvages' dance in Paris. A multi-arm chandelier is suspended from the ceiling, and a pricket candlestick is attached to the chimneypiece. The man to the right appears to be holding a tall candlestick. The tub, used here for extinguishing burning costumes, is a simple bathtub.

Master of the Getty Froissart; Jehan Froissart, Chroniques, Bruges, last quarter of the 15th century, before 1483; British Library, Royal MS 18 E II, fol. 206

ceilings in Gothic buildings. Netherlandish fifteenth-century fireplace corbels mirrored larger architectural corbels supporting window arches or vaulted ceilings. These usually had human head or shield finials (Fig. 5, 10, 37, 125).

Italian Renaissance fireplace consoles also were similar to other consoles that supported large architectural elements. These developed from functional modest scrolled brackets into flamboyant features running from the hood to the floor, which in turn could sometimes be transformed into caryatid-like sculptures.

In England, where fireplaces replaced hearths later than in the rest of Europe, hoods and corbels were generally not installed. Instead, English fireplaces were built flush

to the wall. Such a fireplace form appears to be illustrated in a fifteenth-century English miniature of St Edmund's birth in John Lydgate's *Metrical Lives of Saints Edmund and Fremund* (Fig. 76).

The hood could be considerably reduced or eliminated if, instead of being placed against the wall, the chimneypiece was inserted partially or completely into it. This type of fireplace incorporated entirely into the wall was very fashionable in late fifteenth-century Italy, and the architect and author Scamozzi called it *alla Romana*. Such a fireplace, decorated with the Medici arms, is depicted in a manuscript dated 1502 and was probably commissioned on the occasion of the wedding of Laudomia de' Medici to Francesco Salviati (Fig. 7).

A built-in, or encompassed, fireplace looked like just another rectangular opening in the wall, and an architect such as Serlio could easily frame it with a surround that harmonised with other masonry in doorways and windows, and with the other architectural elements and furniture in the room. An interesting non-Italian example of an encompassed fireplace can be seen on the altar of St Mary's church in Kraków, where a panel shows an elegant chimneypiece, late Gothic in style, in an urban bedroom that serves as the setting for the birth of the Virgin; the chimneypiece matches in its design the doorway in the Annunciation panel of the same altarpiece. This type of *en-suite* decoration on the masonry surrounds of fireplaces, doorways and windows, and sometimes even smaller wall-niches, was quite frequent in Poland.

FIREPLACE ACCESSORIES

Mention should also be made of another type of indispensable furnishing, the fireplace accessories. Metal hooks for cauldrons fixed above hearths were installed in kitchens and in rooms used for cooking or warming up food, and other implements were usually found around fireplaces: firedogs – metal rests for logs – and fire-irons, consisting of a shovel, a billet-hook, a poker and tongs. Iron fire-backs were added to this ensemble relatively late, since they came into use in the sixteenth century. Supplementary elements, such as rests for spits and cooking utensils, were also necessary and normally kept next to kitchen fireplaces. The sets of metal furnishings were often *en suite* and normally of iron, though the more decorative ones were of bronze, either polished or gilded, or damascened. These were sometimes so spectacular that sixteenth-century Venetian sumptuary laws forbade their use. The most decorative of these were the firedogs, which were used in pairs and

[76]
Birth of St Edmund. The royal bedroom is furnished with a large bedstead with textile hangings, and a buffet. The fireplace is truly magnificent and, typically for England, built flush to the wall. The floor is tiled with green glazed tiles and carpeted with a costly rug. Though it is not made clear in the miniature, one can assume that in this high-status room the wall is decorated with a real tapestry and not with a mural painted imitation.

John Lydgate, *Metrical Lives of Saints Edmund and Fremund*, in the presentation copy for Henry VI, England (Bury St Edmunds?), between 1434 and 1439; British Library, Harley MS 2278, fol. 13 v

placed on either side of the hearth (Fig. 5, 6, 34, 53, 67, 76). They were frequently very ornate – one of the Medici inventories lists a fine set bearing the family's arms, which was very fitting, because fireplaces were often decorated with such insignia. Other fireplace accessories and furnishings, such as bellows, chimney-boards and fire-screens, were also vital enhancements.

Bellows were needed to aid the flames on the hearth and are often depicted hanging next to the chimneypiece, mostly in a kitchen or in informal rooms (Fig. 72). More interesting as interior accessories of formal and high-status spaces are the other two types of fittings: chimney-boards and fire-screens.

Chimney-boards are rarely shown in illuminations. An early sixteenth-century Flemish miniature in the Bodleian Library, depicting a truly splendid Gothic fireplace fitted with one, is in this way quite exceptional (Fig. 10). A chimney-board was a major non-masonry element of a fireplace, sealing the chimneypiece when it was not in use. The main purpose of a chimney-board was to exclude draughts and to keep soot or unpleasant smells away from the room. It not only closed off the fireplace tightly but was often also very impressive and decorative. Chimney-boards are documented in several inventories, mainly Italian, and are visible in a few Flemish fifteenth-century paintings. It is not quite clear how they were fixed in place, but some clues are given in the depiction of beautifully crafted chimney-boards by Rogier van der Weyden in the central panel of his Annunciation Triptych, and by Barthélemy d'Eyck's canvas of the Holy Family in Le Puy cathedral. Both paintings suggest that a chimney-board was kept in place by means of metal bolts, permanently fastened to the chimney-board which, when it was inserted into the fireplace, slotted into corresponding apertures in the masonry.

Fire-screens were used to protect people sitting in front of a lit fire from excessive heat and sparks. They were usually broad and high enough to protect one or two seated individuals. In Flanders, France and England they were especially needed because benches were often placed directly in front of chimneypieces (Fig. 20, 70, 71, 125, 126).

Fire-screens could be made of wickerwork or of pierced wood. Several paintings and illuminations show them in quite good detail. Wicker fire-screens can be seen in the January feast scenes in the Duc de Berry's Très Riches Heures, in the Dunois Hours and in other French manuscripts (Fig. 71, 81, 125), and a similar one is depicted in the fifteenth-century panel painting *The Virgin and Child before a Firescreen* by a follower of Robert Campin (now in the National Gallery in London). A wooden pierced screen is depicted on the January page of the Grimani Breviary and the February page of the Golf Book (Fig. 70, 126). The Grimani Breviary fire-screen is particularly attractive and carved with Gothic tracery. The Golf Book fire-screen is much plainer, and looks very similar to the fire-screens depicted in the Master of Flémalle's paintings, for instance in the Mérode Altarpiece.

STOVES

Closed wood-burning stoves originated north of the Alps in the high Middle Ages. The earliest examples of stoves were very simple: small, rounded and not tiled. Towards the end of the Middle Ages, these developed into very large rectangular fire-boxes consisting of a free-standing tiled 'tower' on supports or legs (Fig. 77).

Probably around 1200, untiled stoves started to be covered in so-called *Topfkacheln* (pot tiles). These tiles were made of earthenware, looked like simple bowls and were produced on a potter's wheel. The first tiles were applied to stoves not for decoration but to increase the heating surface of the oven. These were still unglazed and undecorated but this changed over time. The earliest glazes were yellow or green but by the early sixteenth century polychrome lead glazes were applied to stove tiles. The form and the method of production of stove tiles also changed. From the fifteenth century, they were not wheel-turned but moulded, which enabled the inclusion of relief embellishments. These varied widely and could range from the fifteenth-century Gothic architectural elements seen on so-called *Nischenkacheln* (niche tiles), to sixteenth-

[77]
A German interior with a tiled stove.
Note the wooden panelling, the
glazed window typically German in
design, the fixed bench and the tub
for bathing the baby placed in the
warmest corner of the room.

Salomon Trismosin, *Splendor Solis* (an
alchemical treatise), Germany, 1582; British
Library, Harley MS 3469, fol. 31 v

century figurative decorations, which could illustrate scenes from the Bible or from literature and were framed with Renaissance architectural elements. In addition to these,
coats of arms were popular and appeared on stove tiles both in the Middle Ages and in
the Renaissance. The main production centre of moulded stove tiles was the Rhineland
(Germany) with workshops in Cologne, Frechen, Siegburg and Raeren. Rhineland tiles
were not only produced for the local market but were also exported, mostly to the Low
Countries and to England.

Stoves were first used in households in the territories associated with the Hanseatic
League, which was a trading company founded in the thirteenth century. It had trading
posts in several cities on the coasts of the Baltic and the North Sea, and the fashion for
tiled stoves demonstrably followed Hanseatic trade routes. Consequently, tiled stoves
became widespread in the territory that today includes Germany, Austria, Poland, Russia,
Scandinavia and the Baltic states. (See also page 82 for a note on an early depiction of a
stove.) Rarer examples of medieval and Renaissance stoves come from England, France,

the Netherlands, Belgium and the Balkans. There is evidence that stoves were also known and built in other countries, such as Italy, where they were installed mainly in the steam rooms (*stufe*) of bathhouses. Although very popular, wood-burning tiled stoves were very expensive to install and – in times of shortage of wood or in areas where wood was generally scarce – to use. Therefore, outside their primary distribution area, stoves were considered to be a luxury and were installed only in high-status buildings: in royal or aristocratic seats, patrician townhouses or religious establishments.

In the countries of their origin, on the other hand, stoves were commonplace and widespread not only among the nobility but also among the middle classes. However, there were noticeable differences in both the quality and the quantity of the stoves installed in houses of commoners and in residences belonging to the ruling elites. For instance, a sixteenth-century hunting lodge in Knyszyn belonging to the Polish King Zygmunt August is reported to have had tiled stoves and fireplaces not only in most rooms but also in corridors, while the townhouses of rich merchants in Poland's old capital Kraków often had just one stove, though they may have also had additional fireplaces. Similarly, affluent townspeople in German-speaking countries frequently had just one tiled stove. It was a status symbol and therefore located in the best room of the house. Such rooms had a display function and were located on an upper floor and on the main façade side of the house. For insulation they usually had solid timber walls built of logs. Although the interior was often panelled, such rooms were called a *Bohlenstube* (log room). As German townhouses were mostly built in *Fachwerk* (timber frame), the externally exposed log construction of a *Bohlenstube* was immediately recognisable and advertised the wealth of the family, which could afford a stove. Many such log rooms with stoves still exist in Germany and Austria. They can mainly be seen in townhouses but some castles also have them.

A good example of a sixteenth-century German panelled *Bohlenstube* furnished with a very large stove covered in green glazed tiles can be found in several copies of the *Splendor Solis* manuscript. Though the British Library's copy is as late as 1582, earlier copies of the manuscript with the same imagery exist. As the earliest is dated 1532, it can be assumed that the illumination depicting a tiled stove shows an early sixteenth-century interior (Fig. 77).

The construction of stoves such as the one in the *Splendor Solis* illumination was quite ingenious. In German they are called *Hinterladeröfen*, breech-loading stoves. The term applies to stoves which had an opening in an adjacent room, on the other side of a wall. The tiled main body was located in the more formal room while the utilitarian opening was in another, informal room through which the stove could be filled with firewood and ashes could be removed. Constructing stoves in this manner reduced the amount of dust in the room where the family spent their days and received visitors. Since such stoves, even in the Renaissance, often had no chimney, a breech construction helped keep the formal part of the house as smoke-free as possible.

Tiled stoves survive mainly in their primary distribution area but there are also

interesting examples from England and Belgium, where stoves were known, although not widely used, and where they became symbols of sophistication and status.

One of the earliest known English tiled stoves was installed in Whitehall Palace in London. The stove belonged to the royal bathroom: documented in the 1543 palace inventory, it was excavated in 1939. It was commissioned by King Henry VIII, and although it was located in the king's private quarters, its tiles were moulded with royal arms.

In Belgium, tiled stoves are documented in mid-fifteenth-century reception rooms in ducal and aristocratic residences in Bruges, Ghent and Brussels and in a newly built castle at Middleburg. The castle was both an imposing residence and an administrative centre, so it served as a status symbol for the Lords of Middleburg, especially its first owners, Pieter Bladelin and later William Hugonet. Bladelin, who funded not only the construction of the castle but also the erection of a town around it, was, like Hugonet, a *nouveau riche* bourgeois Burgundian court official, and in his attempts to gain noble status and knighthood, he imitated the building programmes and social display patterns of the aristocracy. Above all, the Middleburg castle and its interior decoration were to emphasise and flaunt the newly gained social and political elevation of its owners. The stoves were a part of this scheme and were, in line with their ceremonial purpose, embellished with glazed tiles decorated with symbols of political loyalty and patronage networks, consisting of the personal emblems of the Lords of Middleburg and their allies, and of the heraldry of the Burgundian dukes.

PORTABLE SOURCES OF HEAT

In addition to built-in and mainly architectural sources of heat, portable charcoal-heaters were also a feature of this period. These were very necessary, since of course not all rooms had heating. They were used not only in modest households but also in the best of residences. For instance, many Italian studies were too small to accommodate a fireplace, so an alternative form of heating, preferably portable, had to be used. Such heaters were mostly metal or earthenware containers, and sometimes had pierced tops. These objects are rarely depicted, but a small open-top portable brazier can be seen in an illum-

[78]
Renaissance bakery. A well-appointed and tidy baking house with a decorated oven and a paved floor.
Book of Hours, Bourges, *c.* 1500; Bodleian Library, University of Oxford, MS Canon. Liturg. 99, fol. 16

[79]
Calendar page for September. Making wine on a French estate.
The Dunois Master (associate of the Bedford Master), Book of Hours (The Dunois Hours), Paris, *c.* 1440–*c.* 1450 (after 1436); British Library, Yates Thompson MS 3, fol. 9

[80]
A Florentine fifteenth-century
multipurpose kitchen or dining
room. Kitchens often doubled as
dining rooms. Note the niche with a
lavabo and shelves for vessels above
it. The backrest of the chair standing
next to the *lavabo* has a typically
Tuscan form.

Contrasto di carnesciale et della quaresima,
Florence, c. 1495; British Library, IA.27918

ination of the birth of Alexander in the Bodleian Library's
Romance of Alexander (MS Bodl. 264, pt. 1, fol. 2v).
Braziers came in all sizes – the bigger ones could have
wheels and the smallest ones could be carried about in
winter as hand warmers. Some portable heaters were also
employed as perfume burners or for warming up food, like
the one in the Romance of Alexander miniature.

KITCHENS

It seems that by about 1400 cooking in wealthy European
households had moved to a separate kitchen. Many less
affluent households could not afford extra space for this
luxury or preferred not to banish their sometimes only source of heat to a different room
(Fig. 80, 81).

If a separate kitchen existed, it would most often be located on the ground floor.
Flemish and French illuminations, probably depicting middle-class town or country residences, also indicate that kitchens were placed directly next to a dining room. Some of
them are clearly on the ground floor. Italian fourteenth- and fifteenth-century illuminations in the *Tacuinum sanitatis* show ground-floor country kitchens, often set up under
a type of a loggia. However, we know from surviving inventories, architectural plans
and remains that in townhouses in Italy at this time, kitchens were often placed on top
floors. Apparently this was designed to minimise the threat of fire and to banish cooking
smells from the house.

High-status royal or aristocratic houses had detached kitchen complexes, and Flemish,
Italian and French illuminations depicting country estates often show food preparation
activities such as baking and wine-making taking place in outbuildings (Fig. 26–9, 78,
79). Lesser houses could also use separate buildings for cooking, but the warming up of
food was likely to take place elsewhere. Thus in medieval and Renaissance illuminations
many fireplaces that are possibly in dining rooms or even in bedrooms are shown being
used for simple cooking (Fig. 67, 72, 97).

Most of the time it is difficult to tell, when a meal is depicted being prepared at a fireplace, whether the scene is meant to show a kitchen or another room. However, when
cooking utensils that would normally be stored in a kitchen are absent one can probably
assume that a more formal room is being implied. Meals were frequently prepared away
from kitchens for those who could not leave their bedrooms, such as the sick or new
mothers (Fig. 97). Images of food preparation in a bedroom are frequently found in
Italian decorative art commemorating childbirth and in illuminations showing Nativity
scenes. Also, calendar miniatures illustrating feasting during winter months repeatedly show people at a table in a bedroom being used as a dining room. In such rooms

fireplaces are equipped with metal hooks on which it was possible to hang cauldrons for cooking or warming up food. Wine in metal jugs or in ceramic pots could also be kept warm next to such fireplaces (Fig. 4, 5).

Although illuminations depicting rooms clearly identifiable as kitchens are rare, there are enough to show that fireplaces used primarily for cooking were similar to, though much less ornate than, fireplaces in the more public, formal or ceremonial rooms (Fig. 81).

As well as fireplaces and baking ovens, cooking ranges were in use in higher-status separate kitchens. They became popular in the course of the fifteenth and sixteenth centuries, and are shown mainly in woodcuts and paintings of kitchens in German-speaking states, where they were commonplace.

Not everybody owned a baking oven, and this was especially true of town dwellers and peasants. In winter such ovens would have been a welcome source of heat, but in summer a real nuisance. They also took up a lot of space, used large quantities of fuel and were an additional fire hazard. Ovens were therefore usually located in a separate, free-standing building. At castles or on large country estates ovens could be separated

[81]
A kitchen and neighbouring rooms. The son of Claudius Aesopus, the tragedian, feasts on costly song birds. Miniatures of feasting scenes are very frequent, but illuminations of kitchen interiors are extremely rare.

Attributed to Maître François, Valerius Maximus, trans. by Simon de Hesdin and Nicholas de Gonesse, *Les Fais et les dis des Romains et de autres gens*, Paris, between 1473 and *c.* 1480; British Library, Harley MS 4375, fol. 179

even from kitchens, which were themselves sometimes detached from the living quarters (Fig. 26, 27, 78). In towns and villages communal bakeries were widely used. These either sold their own bread, pastries, pies and cakes, or baked items for clients who brought their pre-prepared, uncooked food to the bakery. Cuts of meat, poultry or sausages were also sent away to be roasted in skillets while kitchen hearths at home were used for roasting on a spit. Even elite families seem to have followed this custom. As stated by Franco Sacchetti in his late fourteenth-century *Il Trecentonovelle*, even the Medici, the then rising stars of Florence, and their betters, used to send their dishes away to town bakeries. This may seem curious, as a near contemporary inventory of 1418 lists not one but two kitchens in the house inhabited by Giovanni de Medici, his sons Cosimo and Lorenzo and their families, before the Palazzo Medici, also in Via Larga, was constructed for Cosimo several decades later (document 'ASF, MaP 129'). The first of these was on the top floor and the second on the ground floor, next to a summer apartment and a kitchen garden. It is possible that installing a private oven was not an option even for a Medici townhouse, but it seemed at times desirable, as sending one's food away to a bakehouse was not without risks. In fact, Sacchetti mentions town bakeries (and sometimes even their Florentine addresses, making it possible even now to reconstruct their location) in conjunction with tales of lamentable loss. In *novella* 186 the writer describes how a servant of Filippo Cavalcanti, the canon of Florence, was robbed of a roast goose stuffed with larks and 'other fat birds' after collecting it from a bakehouse in Piazza de' Bonizi. In another tale, *novella* 124, Sacchetti seems to take personal revenge on his neighbour, Noddo D'Andrea, who was still alive at the time the story was written down and its manuscript lent to the author's friends. Apparently Noddo, a merchant and Sacchetti's father's colleague from Venice, illicitly consumed Sachetti's supper, consisting of two good cuts of meat. Sacchetti reports that his supper was collected from the baker's by a servant by mistake and instead of Noddo's sausages, and that Noddo, ignoring his protesting wife, quickly ate the piping hot roast meat and then handed the skillet – now containing only bare bones – in which the meat had been delivered back to his servant, asking him to run back to the baker's to return it and to collect his own sausages, which he then ate as well. Luckily, Sachetti's tale was not too mean or damaging to Noddo's reputation, which must have been pretty appalling anyway, as he was well known for devouring enormous quantities of hot food with great speed. Sacchetti relates that at banquets Florentines were paired up to share plates and that Noddo was considered a table companion to be avoided at all costs, if one did not want to go home hungry. We meet Noddo again in *novella* 96, which is set around the Rialto market in Venice. Unsurprisingly, this story too deals with food delinquency. Here Noddo and his friends pinch a boiled tripe, which they remove from a pot hanging in a kitchen hearth and replace with an old hat. One can ignore the quality of the typically medieval joke, but it is probably worth noting that the kitchen described here seems to have been on the top floor. It was separate from the room used for dining and was reached by stairs leading up from a merchant's warehouse. The warehouse was probably integrated into the living quarters as a ground floor, and, characteristically for many medieval Venetian merchant houses, it would have had direct access to a canal, which was necessary for handy delivery of goods and convenient for conducting business.

Finally, one has to be aware that illuminations which might appear to be quite useful, as they represent kitchens in connection with contemporary historical events involving royalty, can be deceptive and do not depict the dining hall and kitchen arrangements necessary for complex royal or aristocratic ceremony and refined table etiquette as described in household ordinances. It is apparent that illuminators of these miniatures, as well as of many others, used artistic licence and in fact showed imagined interiors, or those from lower-class households, such as they might be familiar with personally. Examples include an illumination of the Duke of Lancaster dining with the King of Portugal, where the serving hatch is directly next to the high table; as we know from ordinances, this is very unlikely ever to have happened in reality (British Library, Royal MS 14 E IV, fol. 244v).

A number of medieval and Renaissance ordinances and documents describing kitchens have survived, and from them we know quite a lot about how royal and noble households were catered for and fed. Some historic kitchens can still be visited, such as the one at Hampton Court, one of Henry VIII's most elaborate and extensive kitchen complexes. Several other medieval and Renaissance kitchens serving a court or a royal family have been excavated and provide us with further insight into their layout and function.

The organisation and the architectural form of English royal kitchens changed little over several centuries: Tudor kitchens were arranged in a very similar way to their medieval predecessors, up until the time of Henry VIII. The Black Book, Edward IV's household ordinance of 1318, does not differ much from early Tudor ordinances. The changes introduced in household regulations by Henry VIII were a result of the introduction of a more complex royal ceremony and refined table etiquette.

Royal kitchens were very complicated large operations consisting of many specialised offices and feeding several hundred courtiers. They were not normally based in the same building as the lodgings but were separated, some of them more remote than others. This was due to two factors: first, risk of fire, and second, the removal of less pleasant food preparation jobs to the outskirts of the palace quarters.

The scale of food preparation in a royal palace can be illustrated by the kitchen offices in Henry VIII's times. The kitchen department was headed by the lord steward, whose duty was to feed the king and his court. At the beginning of the sixteenth century this meant the preparation of two meals per day for about 800 to 1000 courtiers and other occupants. When the court resided in one of the main royal houses, there were about nineteen kitchen 'offices' (departments) and only one of them was the actual kitchen: the great kitchen (supplying food for the courtiers). However, there were also individual privy kitchens, which operated separately from the great kitchen and provided food and cooked only for the king and his family. Just to list a few, some of the other kitchen offices were: bakehouse, pantry, cellar, buttery, pitcher-house, spicery, boiling-house, larder, poultry, scalding-house and pastry. At greater Tudor houses, each office had its own designated accommodation. During the progress of the court and when it occupied more modest royal houses, some offices could be merged, so that their staff prepared different types of food in the reduced number of kitchen rooms available.

The layout of royal kitchens was governed by efficiency and security. Preparing meals for a very large number of occupants and guests meant that kitchens had to be organised to run smoothly and the different food-preparation tasks had to be specialised and separated from one another. As food was a valuable commodity, especially imported spices and exotic fruit, kitchen staff were constantly supervised to make sure they were not pilfering. Many kitchen rooms were arranged in such a way that food could travel only in the desired direction and staff could be closely monitored. For instance, in Hampton Court most of the kitchen rooms were arranged around courtyards and had only one door each, which led to the courtyard itself. At the end of the kitchen complex was the Great Hall, where the meals were served, and at the other end was the kitchen gatehouse, where the managing clerks had their rooms and could check not only all deliveries but also everything that was leaving the kitchen complex.

2. Lighting

Open hearths and fireplaces, apart from providing warmth, brightened up rooms much more than any other source of light in the Middle Ages and the Renaissance. Any additional sources of light were mainly oil lamps and candles at home, and torches and lanterns outdoors. Numerous contemporary examples of all types of oil lamps, candlesticks, rushlights, sconces, chandeliers and lanterns survive in many museums and private collections. Most of these fixtures were depicted in detail in illuminations and in paintings. Extremely realistic examples are shown in fifteenth-century Flemish panel paintings. Many brass table candleholders and metal sconces can be seen in Master of Flémalle's paintings. Exquisite Gothic brass chandeliers can be found in Jan van Eyck's Arnolfini portrait, in Dieric Bouts the Elder's *Altarpiece of the Holy Sacrament* in Sint-Pieterskerk in Leuven, and in the central panel of Rogier van der Weyden's Annunciation Triptych, now in the Louvre.

OIL LAMPS

Oil lamps were used in Europe from Antiquity and up to and throughout the whole period we are considering here. The simplest

[82]
Presentation scene. A bishop is handing over a book commissioned by him to St Ulrich, the patron of Augsburg cathedral. Note the large chandeliers. They are shown in a church but similar lamps were probably also used in elite domestic settings.

Sacramentary (the 'Augsburg Sacramentary'), Augsburg, second or third quarter of the 11th century; British Library, Harley MS 2908, fol. 8

[83]
The Last Supper in a Renaissance interior. Christ and his apostles are seated around a table in the middle of a room lit by two oil lamps suspended from the ceiling. In the background is a large Italian-style *credenza*, a tiered cupboard, covered with dishes and vessels. The table, benches and the *credenza* are sturdy pieces of furniture and must have been firmly fixed in place. This interior is therefore likely to have been used solely as a dining room, which was still quite rare at the beginning of the sixteenth century but gradually became fashionable across Europe in the following decades.

Vincenzo Raimondi, Book of Hours (Hours of Eleonora Ippolita Gonzaga), Italy (Urbino or Mantua?), 1527 or earlier; Bodleian Library, University of Oxford, MS Douce 29, fol. 56

ones were of clay. These were usually pressed in moulds and decorated with fashionable motifs. Other more expensive oil lamps were made of metal, often copper alloy. Antique forms of lamps enjoyed a revival in the Renaissance, especially in Italy, where bronze oil lamps were very popular as a standard piece of equipment in a scholar's study. Such lamps were not used merely for practical purposes. As they frequently took on elaborate forms and were decorated with historiated motifs, their owners displayed them proudly as collection items. This type of oil lamp was either placed directly on a table or suspended from a metal stand.

Other types of popular oil lamps were conical in shape and made of clay or glass, which was much more costly but translucent. These could be suspended from a stand, inserted in a bracket or a rack fixed to a wall, or hung below the ceiling. Fixtures supporting ceiling lights could be quite complex. A simple suspension consisting of cords or chains would suffice, but in higher-status interiors especially, a richly decorated

massive metal frame could be used. Such fittings could accommodate several individual lamps and, when polished, reflected and intensified the light (Fig. 17, 82, 83).

CANDLES

In the later Middle Ages and in the Renaissance, candles became as popular as oil lamps. They were made either from expensive beeswax or, much more often, from cheap tallow or other types of kitchen fat. They were generally inserted into candleholders. Richer households also used chandeliers, which were luxury items (Fig. 84).

CANDLEHOLDERS

Cheap and small table candleholders were made of clay. These were often glazed and could be decorated. More expensive ceramic candleholders, although still small, were made of maiolica. Other candleholders were made of metal: iron or copper alloys, especially bronze and brass. Tall candlesticks, placed directly on the floor, were also made of metal. These were mainly used in high-status ecclesiastical and secular buildings, though medieval and Renaissance illuminations predominantly show them in depictions of church interiors. The appearance and decoration of tall candlesticks changed over the ages and there were regional variations in their looks, but their rudimentary form remained the same. They could be up to about shoulder-height and they normally catered for a single large candle. A tall metal candlestick for one candle can be seen in a royal bedroom in a fourteenth-century illumination and in much later fifteenth- and sixteenth-century French, Italian and Flemish illuminations showing both secular and ecclesiastical interiors (Fig. 99).

Metal candleholders that could be placed on a dining table or a writing desk were very popular and treasured. Some could accommodate two or three candles. Several excellent examples of these can be seen in the fifteenth-century Turin-Milan Hours illumination showing the birth of St John the Baptist (Fig. 1). Later forms of brass table candleholders accommodating only one candle are shown in the Golf Book, in the February scene illumination, and in Pierre Sala's manuscript (Fig. 70, 84).

Sconces were another kind of candleholder. These were mainly Gothic iron pricket sconces and Renaissance brass sconces, of similar construction, both of which could be ornamented according to fashion. Gothic sconces were usually attached to chimney hoods or to other upper parts of fireplace surrounds, and examples can be seen in Flemish fifteenth-century illuminations and panel paintings (Fig. 74). The Renaissance variant of this type of candleholder can be seen fixed to interior walls in many illuminations of the Polish Behem Codex, which was completed at the beginning of the sixteenth century (Fig. 85). Both of these types of sconces were hinged to vertical surfaces, so that they could be moved according to where the light was needed. At the end of the fifteenth century a completely different, new form of brass sconce, with a round, highly polished back-plate, came into fashion north of the Alps. These were mainly attached to

[84]
A brass candleholder on a Gothic table. The table is covered with a tablecloth and stands next to a buffet. The vista indicates that this room is likely to be in a castle. The walls are faced in stone or painted in imitation, and the floor is paved with stone slabs. See also page 1.

Miniatures attributed to the Master of the Chronique scandaleuse, Pierre Sala, Petit Livre d'Amour, France, Paris and S. E. (Lyon), first quarter of the 16th century; British Library, Stowe MS 955, fol. 8

[85]
Miniature from the Kraków Statutes of the Carpenters. A carpenter's workshop. Note the beautiful *lavabo* niche with a long towel next to it, the metal candleholder and the Gothic cupboard on the wall.

Codex picturatus Balthasaris Behem, Kraków, early 16th century; Biblioteka Jagiellońska, Kraków, MS 16, fol. 290 (original foliation: 284)

[86]
Christ before Caiaphas. The room is lit by a row of sconces.

Attributed to the Master of the Flemish Boethius, Jean Aubert, La Vie de notre seigneur Jhesucrist, La Vengance de la mort Jhesu Christ, Ghent, 1479; British Library, Royal MS 16 G III, fol. 141

chimney-hoods, or placed above the door. They too accommodated just one candle but the polished surface of the back-plate enhanced the brightness of the flame and illuminated the room intensely with glimmering reflected light. One of the earliest depictions of such sconces can be seen in Hieronymus Bosch's panel *Seven Deadly Sins*, dated c. 1480 and now in the Museo del Prado in Madrid. Flemish manuscript illuminations of the beginning of the sixteenth century also depict these, for instance the Beatty Rosarium now in the Chester Beatty Library in Dublin and in the British Library's Hours of Joanna I of Castile (Fig. 65, 75).

Timber, despite being flammable and not the best material to have near to an open fire, was also used to make candleholders. In one of the British Library's fifteenth-century Flemish illuminations, we see a timber bracket in the form of a shelf affixed to a wall and holding several candles (Fig. 86).

CHANDELIERS

By far the most spectacular and costly type of candleholder was the brass chandelier. It was a Flemish speciality, much admired, and exported to other European countries. Brass chandeliers consisted of several arms radiating out from a central support, each of which held one or more candles. Chandeliers were fashionable over several centuries, and their shape and decoration evolved from Gothic to Renaissance, though their essential form remained largely unchanged. They were suspended by strong cords from the ceiling and it was possible to pull them down to blow out the light and to change candles (Fig. 10,

87). They appear in astonishing detail in many paintings of wealthy households; however, the chandelier depicted by Jan van Eyck in the Arnolfini Portrait seems to show one of the most spectacular and costly status symbols, proudly exhibited by an Italian merchant trading from Bruges. An interesting letter from Tommaso Portinari to Piero de Medici also gives evidence of how valued Flemish chandeliers were in fifteenth-century Europe. The document reveals the details of how an exquisite chandelier, intended to adorn one of the Medici houses, was to be shipped to Italy, and describes its beauty and complicated construction.

A completely different type of a chandelier was fashionable in the same period in German-speaking countries. It took the form of a so-called *Leuchterweibchen,* a grotesque female figure, often a bust, resting on a set of antlers. These curious-looking objects do not seem to have been depicted in illuminations but are shown in other contemporary illustrations. One of them is a panel painting of Cardinal Albrecht of Brandenburg as St Jerome in his study, executed by Lucas Cranach in 1526 (now in the Ringling Museum of Art, Sarasota).

Yet another type of chandelier took the form of wooden fittings, and these seem to have been used mainly in loggias and temporary structures. They consisted of planks set in a cross, with bowls for candles at the end of each arm. Just like other chandeliers,

they were suspended from the ceiling by means of a system of cords. Good examples of such temporary chandeliers are depicted in the surviving copies of King René's *Livre des Tournois* and in one of the illuminations of Wodehouses' dance (Fig. 74).

RUSHLIGHTS

Rushlights were an alternative method of lighting. Cheaper than candles, they were very popular, especially in poorer rural dwellings, throughout the Middle Ages and the Renaissance. They consisted of dried rushes dipped in grease or tallow. Usually they were held in metal clips attached to wooden stands or iron tripods. The quality of light given off by rushlights varied depending on the type of substance they were dipped in. They were especially popular in the British Isles and many metal rushlight fittings have survived in collections. Alas, unlike candles, they do not seem to have been interesting enough to be depicted in illuminations.

TORCHES AND LANTERNS

Torches and lanterns typically provided light out of doors. In the Golf Book illumination of the February feast, we can see torches brought in by men taking part in the festivities (Fig. 70). Lanterns, which had metal frames and were often fitted with translucent

[88]
St Luke in his study. Note the lantern on the lectern.

The Bedford Master, Book of Hours (The Bedford Hours), Paris, *c*. 1423–30; British Library, Add. MS 18850, fol. 20 v glass panels, so much safer than torches, were frequently used not only outdoors but also as permanent indoor fixtures. They could be used in a variety of ways. In Flemish illuminations they are seen used as large chandeliers suspended from ceilings. In French manuscripts they are shown as small desk lamps attached to metal stands (Fig. 88).

3. Hygiene

Contrary to the popular belief that the Middle Ages were a time of absolute squalor and grime, medieval hygiene was more advanced than that in the following centuries. Alas, in the sixteenth century, bathing started to go out of fashion, as it was thought to cause diseases. In Europe it was not until the nineteenth century that standards of hygiene returned to fifteenth-century levels.

BATHING AT HOME

Private bathrooms existed in royal and other elite houses in medieval and Renaissance northern and southern Europe. For instance, there are accounts of bathrooms and steam rooms in the thirteenth-century Tower of London, in sixteenth-century Westminster Palace and in the fifteenth-century ducal palace in Ferrara. Many houses of this class had running water, led through pipes to taps. Sometimes water was heated and came out of the tap warm. Indeed, it was not only elite palaces that had running water. Middle-class households in cities had access to such luxury as well. For a fee, it was possible to have your house connected to the municipal conduit. Many houses in Italy, and especially in Venice, also had their own underground rain-water cisterns (Fig. 47). Poorer town dwellers had to use private or a communal fountains connected to the conduits, and these were mostly a necessary, rather than purely decorative, feature needed to regulate excess water (Fig. 32, 89). Excess water was also used to flush out lavatories and sewers. Although the sophisticated plumbing technology existed, and the remains of such luxuries have not only survived but are documented in archives, they were expensive and relatively rare among the lower classes, who had to rely on wells or cisterns as a water supply, and on cesspits instead of sewers.

Instead of private bathrooms, most classes usually had a bathtub brought into the (bed)room or, at best, to an adjacent room. The tub was made on the same principle as a

[89]
Calendar page for April. Flemish castle complex buildings and a garden with a fountain.

Simon Bening and workshop, Book of Hours (Golf Book), Bruges, probably early 1540s; British Library, Add. MS 24098, fol. 21 v

 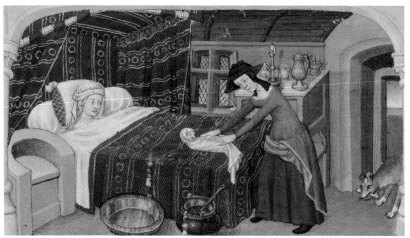

barrel and was either open or covered with a lid with a cut-out in the middle, or with a pavilion, to keep the steam in. The tub could be lined with a sheet before one got in. Water was normally brought in from the well outside and warmed up in cauldrons on the fire. Many illuminations and woodcuts depict bathing scenes (Fig. 90). It seems that there were also numerous Flemish paintings showing ladies bathing in their bedrooms, possibly similar to a panel depicting Bathsheba at her bath and executed in 1485 by Memling (Staatsgalerie, Stuttgart). One such painting was attributed to Jan van Eyck. Now lost, it is documented by Willem van Haecht's panel of 1628 showing it displayed in the gallery of Cornelis van der Geest (this work is now in the Rubenshuis in Antwerp, Belgium). A presumed sixteenth-century copy of van Eyck's picture, *Woman at Her Bath*, still exists (now in Harvard Art Museums/Fogg Museum, Cambridge, Massachusetts). These images must have been very popular abroad as well, as Florentine fifteenth-century accounts mention imported Flemish canvases of this sort. Most of these are likely to have been destroyed in Savonarola's bonfire of the vanities in 1497.

However, the bathing scenes in illuminations are mainly birth depictions, which show preparations for babies' baths. It seems that in the fifteenth and sixteenth centuries in

[90]
A public bathhouse. The bathroom is located next to bedrooms, where one could rest after ablutions. Such rooms gave these establishments a bad reputation and caused their closure. Note the plain planked door and a cloth-lined bathtub.
Rambures Master, Valerius Maximus, *Le livre de Valerius Maximus* (*Facta et dicta memorabilia*, translated by Simon de Hesdin and Nicholas de Gonesse), France (Amiens or Hesdin) or Flanders, third quarter of the 15th century; British Library, Royal MS 17 F IV, fol. 297

[91]
A new mother and her baby in a bedroom. New-born babies were bathed in wooden or metal tubs. Birth scenes often depict water being warmed up in a fireplace for the baby's first bath. Here a cauldron of water with a ladle is placed next to the tub.
Attributed to the Master of the Royal Alexander, *Le Livre et le vraye hystoire du bon roy Alixandre* (*Historia de proelis*, trans. into French), Paris, c. 1420; British Library, Royal MS 20 B XX , fol. 86 v

[92]
Dining al fresco. The wine cooler looks similar to contemporary bathtubs (see Fig. 49).
Salomon Trismosin, *Splendor Solis* (an alchemical treatise), Germany, 1582; British Library, Harley MS 3469, fol. 28

French and Italian polite circles, timber bath tubs were replaced by more elegant, metal tubs. This fashion can be observed in several illustrations (Fig. 49, 91). Some of these tubs must have been multipurpose, as one is used as a wine cooler in the garden scene from the German *Splendor Solis* manuscript (Fig. 92).

PUBLIC BATHS, COSMETICS AND MEDICINE

Not everybody had their own bedroom and not everybody wanted to bathe at home. Numerous bathhouses were therefore provided in most cities across medieval Europe. They were frequented sometimes several times a week and considered both a necessity and a healthy pleasure. Unfortunately, during the fifteenth century they started to gain a bad reputation, mainly because of associated prostitution, and most of them were closed in the sixteenth century. Some illuminations record this type of scandalous bathhouse, where the rows of bathtubs were supplemented by beds in adjacent rooms (Fig. 90).

Barber-surgeons and apothecaries, sometimes working on the premises of bathhouses, were also at hand and provided cosmetics, medicines and health advice (Fig. 30, 93, 109). Their services were available to all but the poorest. Some of their knowledge has survived in manuscripts such as the *Tacuinum sanitatis* and calendars of books of hours.

EWER AND BASIN SETS AND LAVABOS

Apart from bathtubs, shown mostly in Nativity scenes, vessels for hand-washing are frequently depicted, mainly in Annunciation scenes. Numerous Flemish paintings depict beautiful ewer and basin sets in lavabo niches or on dressers. A mid-fifteenth-century Flemish illumination of the Annunciation from the Llangattock Hours picks up this tradition (Malibu, J. Paul Getty Museum, MS. Ludwig IX 7, fol.53v). In these images hand-washing sets were symbols of Mary's purity, but their depictions were based on real objects and the frequent use of them at home. Similar objects are also seen on secular images of prosaic interiors such as kitchens, artisan workshops, bedrooms and studies, and they must have been used by most classes (Fig. 80, 85, 94, 140).

4. Beds and bedrooms

BEDROOMS

Bedrooms as we know them came into existence in the lower ranks of society very gradually and are not well documented. Royal, noble and middle-class European bedrooms, on the other hand, are best described in inventories. There are numerous descriptions of medieval and Renaissance English royal private quarters and bedrooms in the Tower of London, at Hampton Court and at many other residences. This development seems to have been similar in other north European countries. However, contemporary images of them are very rare, although their architectural shell often survives. Partially surviving bedrooms of the nobility and the middle classes in Italy, therefore, with their associated furniture, inventories, account books and imagery (such as paintings, frescoes or illuminations) are particularly useful. Charming surviving early bedroom examples can be found in Tuscany, such as in the Casa Datini in Prato, dating from the late fourteenth and early fifteenth century. However, one has to bear in mind that the majority of extant historical interiors have been heavily restored and that their furniture often comes from another context, as is the case in the Palazzo Davanzati in Florence.

Middle and upper-class Tuscan bedrooms, and especially in Florence in the late medieval and Renaissance periods, were especially sophisticated and celebrated the importance of the power of family in civic ambitions. Tuscan bedrooms were usually in the most private area of the house. The main and the most elaborate furniture piece here was the bedstead, which created a functional whole with other bedroom furnishings. The bedstead, wedding chests and boxes were the essential commodities of this room. Other pieces of furniture and objects typical as bedroom equipment were daybeds, devotional images, mostly of Virgin Mary, and painted birth-trays, decorated and commemorating newborn children, and sometimes displayed like paintings on the wall. The walls of Tuscan elite bedrooms were embellished with frescoes or wall hangings. The walls and furniture were often enhanced with symbolic decoration aimed at the encouragement of piety and of civic virtues. Heraldic decoration played an important role in displaying and affirming political aspirations even in this private setting. Along with the often costly furniture, a large part of the family's valuables and other possessions were stored here. Valuables were not only needed to improve the family's living standards, they also had a symbolic meaning and expressed their owners' refined taste, wealth, political bonds and dynastic ambitions. These values were also displayed elsewhere in the house, chiefly in the halls and studies, and of course the exterior of the building and its architectural design also made a public statement of the same values and messages.

MATTRESSES

Four-poster beds are generally associated with the Middle Ages and the Renaissance. In fact, they developed relatively late. Like most other furniture pieces, they rarely survive but the earliest descriptions and depictions of beds of this kind come from the last decades of the fifteenth century and were executed in northern Italy. If the grand four-poster beds seen as typical of the Middle Ages did not exist until the late fifteenth century, what did their ancestors look like and what were the contemporary simpler alternatives?

A mattress filled with hay, horse-hair or wood chips was the most frequent type of medieval bed for both the poorest and wealthier Europeans. In the majority of households, even bedrooms were a luxury and inhabitants had to sleep in multifunctional rooms, which at night served as bedrooms for family and servants alike. In the morning the mattresses were rolled up and stored so that the room could be transformed into a living room, a workshop or, in grander settings – in English castles and manor houses, for example – as a great hall.

[95]
Dormitory with narrow beds.

John Lydgate, *The Pilgrimage of the Life of Man*, England (West Suffolk?), *c.* 1430–50; British Library, Cotton Tiberius MS A. VII, fol. 99

[96]
A king in his narrow but decorative bed.

Bestiary, with extracts from Giraldus Cambrensis on Irish birds, England (Salisbury?), 2nd quarter of the 13th century; British Library, Harley MS 4751, fol. 40

[97]
The blinding of Tobit. Tobit is resting on a possible daybed or settle. A fabric hanging decorates the wall behind him. A meal is being cooked in the same room. The simple turned stool is Flemish. The wooden floor is particularly well depicted.

Master of the Soane Josephus and Master of Edward IV, Guyart des Moulins, *La Bible historiale*, volume 4 (*Bible historiale* of Edward IV), Bruges, 1470–c. 1479; British Library, Royal MS 15 D I , fol. 18

SIMPLE WOODEN FRAMED BEDS

Wooden framed beds, even simple ones, were expensive and took up valuable space. Some of them could be quickly dismantled and consisted of a board on trestles, probably very similar to contemporary tables. There are many references to such beds in Italian inventories, though by the fifteenth century they were considered to be of an old type and out of fashion – not surprising, as such structures must have been very unstable, wobbly and uncomfortable. A sturdier alternative to such a simple bed was a narrow board framed with upright planks and propped up on square wooden blocks projecting from its corners. These often feature in images showing patients in beds. In hospitals or at home, narrow unfussy beds have always been practical when nursing the sick. Very good examples of such bed frames with their simple bedding are shown in an English illumination executed c. 1430–50, in a copy of John Lydgate's *Pilgrimage of the Life of Man*,

[98]

The birth of the Virgin Mary in a
Polish city interior. The room is
furnished with Gothic-style furniture.
The narrow, single bed and a cradle
stand in the middle. The table has
a northern European form. A small
cupboard with doors hangs on the
wall and there is a chest or bench
underneath. The floor is paved with

heavy tiles, which were common on
ground floors. Another indication
of a ground-floor location are grille
inserts in the windows, which were
installed for protection.

Pontifikal Erazma Ciolka, Kraków, early 16th
century; Princes Czartoryski Foundation,
Kraków, RKPS 1212, fol. 23 (detail)

[99]
King Eralac and his chamberlain
in a royal bedroom.

*Estoire del Saint Graal, La Queste del
Saint Graal, Morte Artu*, France (Saint-
Omer or Tournai?), first quarter of the
14th century; British Library, Royal
MS 14 E III, fol. 11 v

a translation of Guillaume Deguileville's *Pèlerinage de vie humaine* (Fig. 95). The beds are arranged side by side in a large dormitory, a setup suitable for pilgrims or for the sick. The dormitory is looked after by a woman smoothing the bedding with a stick. This interesting detail of the miniature adds to our understanding of how beds were made, though probably such long sticks must have been more useful for very large bedsteads.

The basic narrow bed form, still in use in the sixteenth century, existed for hundreds of years across Europe, was used by all classes, and could be quite elaborate and decorative if made for the social elite. Narrow ornamental beds of this type can be seen in British Library illuminations from a twelfth-century German lectionary and a thirteenth-century English bestiary (Fig. 17, 96). The Nativity scene in the lectionary depicts Mary in a simple bed with legs and finials turned on a lathe. Beds of this type were in use in the area where the manuscript was produced for at least half a millennium: a seventh-century bed excavated in the same region of Germany looked very similar. The English bestiary illumination shows a Caladrius bird sitting at the bedside of a king. The bed is very narrow but beautifully carved and painted and has four turned posts that serve as legs and finials. The backrest is an added bonus and makes the piece of furniture look like a daybed, which may be what we see in a Flemish illumination of the late fifteenth century (Fig. 97). Although daybeds were evidently known in northern Europe, they were probably more popular in Italy, as surviving examples and inventory entries suggest. A Nativity scene in the Polish early sixteenth-century *Pontifical of Erazm Ciolek* also depicts a simple, single bed (Fig. 98). Although the bed occupied by Mary is narrow and gives easy access to the new mother, it is beautifully made: its side panels are elegantly carved in Gothic style and the legs and finials of the bed are turned on a lathe and gilded.

Medieval beds are often depicted almost completely covered with bedding, piled-up pillows and sheets, which makes it very difficult to make out the details of the bed itself. Many beds seem to have been not only single and narrow but also very short, so that people shown on them sometimes look almost wedged in and uncomfortable. This bed construction must have been deliberate as sleeping in a sitting position was favoured at the time. These unassuming beds are often shown surrounded by curtains. Most of the time the curtains look detached from the bed frame and are suspended from a single straight rod (Fig. 99).

BEDSTEADS

More elaborate fourteenth-century French and northern Italian beds often share the same feature: a very tall, curved headboard. Such beds could be quite large and their headboards were decorated. At first they were accompanied by benches and later by chests (Fig. 100–102).

In fifteenth-century Italy the chests surrounding the bed on three sides were integrated into the bedstead and produced as one gigantic furniture unit with straight, corniced headboards (Fig. 7). Inventories also indicate that Italian elites used to

[106]
Henry VIII praying in his Renaissance bedchamber. This room is probably imaginary but must have been based on elements of Tudor interiors. Note the four-poster bed.

Jean Mallard (illuminator and scribe), Psalter ('The Psalter of Henry VIII'), London, c. 1540–1; British Library, Royal MS 2 A XVI, fol. 3

[107]
St Luke in his study. The study has a bedroom entrance at the back. The evangelists are usually shown in their studies. Here St Luke inhabits a splendidly furnished French Renaissance suite consisting of a study with a spacious bedroom. The study has a typically French buffet, also seen in bedrooms and halls, and the bedroom has a four-poster bed, which was a novelty at the time of the production of this manuscript.

In the style of Jean Pichore, *Explication des actes des apôtres*, Paris, c. 1510; British Library, Harley MS 4393, fol. 6 v

in an illumination in the British Library's Psalter of Henry VIII. It was produced in London in *c.* 1540–1 and written and illuminated by Jean Mallard, a French court poet to Henry VIII and previously to the King of France, Francis I (Fig. 106). The illumination shows Henry VIII praying in his bedroom. The king owned numerous palaces in which he resided on a regular basis and it is possible that both the depicted bedroom and the building in which it is set existed but so far they have not been identified. It is very probable that the architecture and associated interiors shown in Henry VIII's manuscript are in fact imaginary. This seems to be a justified assumption, especially since Henry VIII's illuminator seems to have based some of the furnishings depicted on the ones

illustrated in *Hypnerotomachia Polifili*, which was a fashionable publication and must have been known in English and other court circles. The action in the book takes place in a dream, and it sometimes describes and illustrates idealised or fantastic versions of luxury settings. Such fantastic versions of the latest current fashions might not have belonged to mere mortals, but could have been owned by monarchs, who had the best designers, carpenters and joiners at their disposal. Henry VIII's bed in Mallard's illumination is a gigantic box-like bedstead taking up most of the visible interior. It has a sturdy panelled base supported on intricately carved legs. Similar legs are shown on *Hypnerotomachia Polifili* beds and chests, and on a chest or a desk in another illumination from the Psalter showing Henry VIII with his jester in a lavish garden loggia (Fig. 110). The posts of Henry VIII's bedstead are turned on a lathe and the decorative details could have been carved and gilded. Dark blue valances and curtains are embellished with gold thread embroidery and tassels. The fabrics are held up by a tester supported by the posts and stretching over the entirety of the wooden base of the bed. The mattress seems to be topped with thick soft bedding and covered with a red velvet or silk bedspread.

Even though the particular details of the bedstead in Mallard's illuminations could have been imaginary, posted beds became extremely fashionable all over sixteenth-century Europe and they stayed in fashion in the following centuries. Some of the examples were very elaborate and costly, being designed and produced by professionals. Initially only the elites could afford them but gradually they became attainable to other sections of society.

Another early posted bedstead can be seen in a manuscript illuminated *c.* 1510 in Paris (Fig. 107). The folio showing St Luke as a scholar in his study gives a glimpse into a bedroom furnished with a handsome four-poster bedstead. Its side panels are decorated with linenfold carvings.

5. Chests, Cupboards and Shelves

Wooden chests were the most popular pieces of medieval and Renaissance storage furniture, especially in the main living areas – the bedroom, the hall and the study – but they were not very frequently depicted. Most of the images showing them are Italian, and scholarship has concentrated mainly on Italian examples. Chests were widely used throughout Europe, and over the centuries there were many regional variations in the form, internal structure and decoration, and the materials from which they were made. Most chests were made from wood and the earliest medieval chests known to us are just very crudely hollowed-out tree trunks. More elaborate ones were finished with more care and their decoration reflected contemporary trends. They could be painted, inlaid with other types of wood, carved and embellished with figurative, floral, geometric or architectural decoration, such as Romanesque blind arcading, Gothic tracery or classically inspired Renaissance motifs.

Cupboards, in all shapes and sizes, were used for storage from Antiquity onwards. They were constructed from the same materials and decorated like chests, but they were clearly less important in the Middle Ages and the Renaissance. Shelving in all forms was universally used for storage and ranged from a basic single board to large, box-like fitted units encountered mainly in studies (Fig. 107).

STORAGE AND SECURITY

Chests would usually be arranged along the walls in halls or next to the bed in bedrooms. They were used for the storage of all sorts of valuables: tableware (silverware and maiolica), linen, books, money, jewellery, documents, family records and so on. Many medieval and Renaissance chests for domestic use were portable, but often big enough to hold unfolded, long clothes. Boccaccio's *Decameron* mentions chests in several tales in connection with people hiding in them, and on a few occasions a person was easily carried in one. These pieces must therefore have been man-size but relatively light. Some chests, even if made for the storage of very large items, had separate compartments for smaller objects, and this is clearly visible in Jan van Eyck's illumination depicting the Birth of St John in the Turin-Milan Hours (Fig. 1).

Chests for valuables were lockable and we can see such locks on many illuminations (Fig. 1, 101, 102, 108, 109, 134). Strongboxes, which had the function of a modern safe, could even have more than one lock. These, for extra security, could only be opened with different keys turned simultaneously by two or more people. They were found in both domestic and institutional contexts. The chest depicted here is a main piece of furniture at an Italian bank (Fig. 108). Documents indicate that a possibly similar secure 'Chest of Five Keys' was used in the fifteenth century at the University of Oxford to keep the university's revenue, accounts and other valuables. Such strongboxes were normally purely utilitarian, made of iron or wood, bound with iron straps and undecorated, though they could be covered with leather.

Large furniture chests were used for storage at home. Smaller coffers or caskets were utilised both at home and as travelling trunks or strongboxes for transporting valuable items on trips. Many larger travelling chests had domed lids to prevent the accumulation of rainwater. Their shape was often modified so that they could be comfortably carried in pairs by an animal, usually a donkey or a mule.

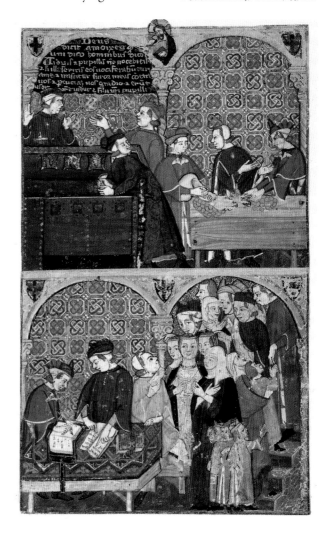

[108]
The interior of a counting house. Note the chest or strongbox.

Master of the Cocharelli Codex, Cocharelli, *Treatise on the Vices*, Genoa, *c.* 1330– *c.* 1340; British Library, Add. MS 27695, fol. 8

[109]
Perfumer's shop. Note the lockable chest and the shelves filled with apothecary's jars and containers.

John Lydgate, *The Pilgrimage of the Life of Man*, England (West Suffolk?), *c.* 1430–50; British Library, Cotton Tiberius MS A. VII, fol. 93

MULTIPURPOSE CHESTS

Most chests, apart from the ones with domed lids, could serve as seats, especially if arranged along walls or beds. Even the free-standing ones were effective seats or even tables, especially in studies, where lockable storage was needed for important paperwork, expensive books and sometimes even scientific instruments or collections of all sorts of curious and/or costly objects (Fig. 43, 107, 110, 134). Some sixteenth-century chests serving as benches might have a comfortable backboard to lean on; in Tuscany they were called *cassapanca*. Other chest-like storage spaces were created inside more elaborate seats covered with hinged lids. One example is the forerunner of today's sofa, the fifteenth-century Italian day-bed (*lettuccio*), which was related in construction to a *cassapanca*. In northern Europe in the fifteenth century, the typical seating furniture offering a similar type of storage space included chairs, settles and benches with fixed or movable backrests (Fig. 10, 11, 97, 111).

Italian bedside chests are a particularly interesting example of multipurpose furniture. They were handy for storage, as seats, as bedside tables and as steps leading up to the bed. They further underwent an unusual development, which occurred only in Italy. Up to the end of the fourteenth century, Italian beds, like beds in other parts of Europe, would typically have one or more detached chests arranged next to them (Fig. 98, 101), which could be made as part of a matching ensemble. In time, sets of bedroom chests were integrated completely with the bed and became its structural components. These massive bedsteads, fixed to the wall at the head and surrounded by elongated storage chests were prevalent in Italy in the fifteenth century but seem not to have been popular anywhere else in Europe (Fig. 7, 102).

CASSONI

A large free-standing chest referred to in modern literature as a *cassone* (although its contemporaries often used other terms to describe it) has drawn a lot of scholarly attention in the last century because of its decorative appeal and the important part it played in Italian, and especially Tuscan, social history. Above all, the painted *cassoni* were studied widely in the context of the highest-quality interior decoration.

Cassoni were very popular in fifteenth-century Tuscany and numerous renowned artists were commissioned to decorate them with historiated scenes. Interesting in this context is the fact that one of the mid-fifteenth-century Florentine workshops, run by Apollonio di Giovanni, produced both manuscript illuminations and painted chests. Not surprisingly, a good example of such a chest in its original context can be seen in Apollonio di Giovanni's 1460s illumination from Virgil's *Aeneid*, showing Dido in her bedroom (Biblioteca Riccardiana, Florence, MS 492, fol. 67v). However, in spite of their great popularity and importance, representations

[110]
Henry VIII playing the harp and his court jester in a Renaissance loggia. Note the chest doubling as table.

Jean Mallard (illuminator and scribe), Psalter ('The Psalter of Henry VIII'), London, c. 1540–1; British Library, Royal MS 2 A XVI, fol. 63 v

[111]
St Luke with the Virgin Mary and St Paul (?). Note the seat with chest-like storage space underneath.

Muzio Attendolo Master, Book of Hours (Hours of Bona Sforza), Milan, c. 1490–4; British Library, Add. MS 34294, fol. 4

of historiated *cassoni* are very rare. In the same manuscript, there are several other examples of chests, but none of them is painted with bright colours or with figurative motifs. For instance, two chests, carved (and possibly inlaid or covered with *pastiglia*?) are shown being transported by Aeneas (fol. 74). In front of Dido's palace, which strongly resembles a Florentine Renaissance *palazzo* (such as the Palazzo Medici), the smaller chest is handed over to Dido as a bridal gift (fol. 74v). Such chests could have been filled with valuable objects – presents from the bridegroom on the occasion of marriage. Another, larger free-standing unhistoriated chest with a domed lid is placed against a wall of Aeneas' bedroom (fol. 81). Dido's and Aeneas's bedrooms are also both furnished with large bedsteads typical of fifteenth-century Tuscany, each surrounded by incorporated chests with flat lids – used, as we have seen, for storage, as seats and as steps to the bed.

The main function of a *cassone* was as a marriage chest – a piece of furniture commissioned by the bridegroom for his betrothed. Such chests were often commissioned in pairs and brought to the bride's house before the wedding ceremony. The bride's family filled the chests with her dowry and with other presents from the groom. The *cassoni* were then paraded in the streets when the newly married woman was leaving her parental home to join her husband, normally in his parents' house. In consequence such chests were usually part of the married couple's bedroom furniture, though other types of chest could also be found elsewhere in their house.

In the fifteenth century, Tuscan marriage chests made especially for the bedroom were usually decorated with paintings or inlaid wood decoration (*tarsie*). The inlay ornament could consist of expensive types of wood or ivory. In the sixteenth century, other types of decoration, such as carving, gained in popularity. Carved chests were usually made of valuable walnut and partially gilded. Some *cassoni* were enhanced with *spalliere*, painted horizontal panels.

Several decades after the fashion for painted *cassoni* faded away, when it became very difficult to find good artists who would take on furniture-decorating commissions, Giorgio Vasari, who was in charge of architectural projects for Cosimo I de' Medici, Grand Duke of Tuscany, praised the fifteenth-century artists who had contributed to *cassoni* decoration. On the other hand, Girolamo Savonarola, a fifteenth-century Dominican friar and influential preacher, criticised Florentines for commissioning artists to paint wedding chests with pagan stories, which did not supply the newly-weds with Christian examples to imitate. In his criticism, Savonarola was referring to the change in taste which took place in the late fifteenth century. Fourteenth-century Tuscan domestic imagery drew mainly on the Bible, on Christian literature and on contemporary and local literary sources such as Petrarch and Boccaccio. The developing Renaissance brought about considerable changes in fashion and fifteenth-century historiated decoration was frequently based on classical literature and mythology. The term employed to describe this new type of iconography was *all'antica*.

According to Tuscan tradition, furniture which was meant to decorate the marital bedroom and private space should have a didactic purpose and carry specific messages inspiring the young couple to lead a virtuous family life and to keep up and develop their private and civic virtues. Thus, the messages conveyed by the fourteenth- and fifteenth-century images aimed at the same purpose but drew on different traditions. The new *all'antica* imagery failed to meet with Savonarola's approval: as a devout and uncompromising friar, Savonarola favoured the Christian tradition and condemned the moral value of classical examples.

Some Tuscan *cassoni*, or parts of them, still survive. The components least likely to perish were the *spalliere*, which, though they have often become detached from the chests, were closely associated with them. *Spalliere* and other highly decorated sections, mostly front boards, of *cassoni* were very much appreciated for their aesthetic value. In consequence, they often became separated from chests and were kept as independent pictures. A number of such painted panels can now be seen displayed on gallery and museum walls. One of the best-known boards associated with fifteenth-century Florentine chests is the so-called Adimari Cassone, probably a *spalliera*, attributed to Scheggia, now in the Galleria dell'Accademia, Florence. However, we have to be aware that panels which are sometimes interpreted as components of *cassoni* or elements associated with them may also have been parts of other types of furniture, mostly bedroom. They could have been displayed over the backboards of *lettucci* (as was Botticelli's *Primavera*), or they could have belonged to horizontal wall panelling or bed-heads. For example, as already mentioned, another famous possible *cassone spalliera,* Botticelli's painting *Venus and Mars* is, according to recent research, possibly more likely to have been associated with a bed or a bench.

CUPBOARDS AND SHELVES

The English word 'cupboard' derives its etymology from a shelf for storage and display of cups and plate. Such pieces of furniture and their more sophisticated variants called *credenzas*, *dressoirs* or buffets, are discussed in the section on tables. Cupboards as we know them – enclosed storage units, often in the form of a box with an opening at its front rather than top (unlike chests) and equipped with doors – were not very frequent in Europe in the Middle Ages and the Renaissance. They supplanted chests and started to gain massive popularity in the sixteenth and seventeenth centuries, and have remained in use since then. The earliest extant cupboards are not easy to date with precision but they are Romanesque in style. However, they are probably of ecclesiastical rather than domestic origin (such as the sacristy cupboard, dated *c.* 1200, in the cathedral treasury at Halberstadt). A few medieval illuminations show large early medieval cupboards filled with books and located in very stylised surroundings functioning as studies (for example, in a portrait of the scribe Ezra from the late seventh century Codex Amianitus (Biblioteca Medicea Laurenziana, Florence, MS Amianitus 1, fol. 5). As these cupboards are in depictions of religious or church personalities, one can assume that they are also representative of a monastic rather than a secular context. Further to this difficulty, there is very little documentary or material evidence of such early furniture and it is uncertain whether there was any distinction between domestic and religious pieces. However, as studies in private secular contexts were still very rare and most scholars and manuscripts would belong to religious institutions at that time, we may perhaps safely assume that both the depictions and the extant pieces were also non-domestic.

The spreading Renaissance fashion for private domestic studies is also reflected in the greater number of illuminations and other depictions of them in European art. This is true mainly of Italy, but studies were also becoming more frequent in northern Europe and can be seen in French, Flemish, German and Polish sources. Even if chests seem still to dominate such spaces as storage furniture, examples of cupboards and open shelving units can also be found there. Some of the simplest cupboards consisted of large or small wall niches filled with shelves and covered by curtains or doors. Several of these built-in constructs can be seen in fifteenth-century Flemish manuscripts (Fig. 43). Contemporary Italian Florentine illuminations often show tall and very plain bookcases, built-in but attached to the wall and open-fronted, which created an *en-suite* and well-designed unit with desks,

[112]
Miniature from the Kraków Statutes of the Shoemakers. A shoemaker's workshop. Note the northern European type table, bentwood chair, bench with a convertible backrest, and shelving unit for shoes. Large cupboards or shelving units like the one shown here were more frequent in shops and workshops than in domestic interiors. In illuminations they are depicted filled with all sorts of merchandise: metalwork, textiles, medicines, cosmetics or pigments.

Codex picturatus Balthasaris Behem, Kraków, early 16th century; Biblioteka Jagiellonska, Kraków, MS 16, fol. 293 (original foliation: 287)

seats and chests. Many of these were made to measure and fitted into often really tiny spaces used as studies. Boxlike cupboards with doors can also be seen in German art, for instance in Cardinal Albrecht of Brandenburg's study painted by Lucas Cranach in 1526. Illuminations show similar simple wall cupboards with doors in bedrooms, workshops and kitchens. Many are decorated with Gothic tracery and crenellations (Fig. 72, 85, 98, 140). One of the most attractive depictions of a large, standing and probably built-in cupboard with an open-fronted bookcase comes from an illumination of St Luke painting the Virgin and Child in a Flemish book of hours dated *c.* 1500 (Fig. 138). Similar cupboards, if much more sophisticated and with upper parts enclosed with latticed doors, are shown in the illusionistic inlaid wall panelling of Duke Federico da Montefeltro's *studioli* in Gubbio (now in the Metropolitan Museum of Art) and in Urbino (still in situ). It is also possible that the built-in cupboards in the Piero and Lorenzo de' Medici study at the Florentine Palazzo Medici were designed in a similar way. However, it is worth noting that large standing cupboards, with or without doors (although they did exist) are quite rarely depicted and are usually shown in institutional rather than domestic interiors, such as workshops, shops and doctors' surgeries or drugstores (Fig. 93, 109, 112, 124).

Single shelves, on the other hand, were truly universal and are encountered in all contexts. They were usually fixed at head-height but can also be seen much higher, for example, above doors (Fig. 1, 72, 86, 103, 107, 113). An alternative to a single shelf was often provided by all sorts of protrusions, such as chimneypieces, cornices and window-sills.

6. Benches, Chairs and Stools

BENCHES

As discussed above, low chests with flat lids tended to be multifunctional and used both for storage and as seats. Such benches doubling up as chests could be arranged around beds or against walls, or set up free-standing in the middle of rooms (Fig. 110, 111).

Probably the most celebrated and iconic northern European bench of the late Middle Ages and Renaissance was a seat that was placed directly in front of the fireplace. Thanks to an adjustable, swinging backrest, which could be moved to the front or to the back of the bench, it was a very practical piece of furniture. Depending on the position of the backrest, one could sit on the bench either facing the fire or looking towards the room. The second option was used mainly in warmer months, when the fire was not lit, or at meals, when tables were set up in front of fireplaces (Fig. 13, 52, 81, 112, 114).

Such swing-back benches were used mainly in Flanders and France, but similar, simplified benches were also known in other countries, mainly in Germany, England and Italy. The most realistic, detailed depictions of their construction, Gothic carving and other embellishments – such as lion-head finials on armrests – are found in the best Flemish fifteenth-century panel paintings showing affluent domestic interiors. Naturally, swing-back and other benches habitually appear together with fireplaces. Many of the best-quality Flemish and French depictions also include them and sometimes show their decoration in detail.

By the beginning of the sixteenth century, Netherlandish swing-back benches had gone out of fashion and been replaced by benches with fixed backrests. In Flanders they were placed with their back to the fire and must have blocked off quite a lot of light. They looked more utilitarian than their predecessors, though their side and front panels could be carved with Gothic or Renaissance ornaments (Fig. 10, 75).

Similar in appearance and construction to these were daybeds, which had wider seats and higher backrests, and were positioned against walls. Painted and carved, elaborate daybeds were typically Italian elite furniture pieces but, in a simpler form, they were also known in other countries (Fig. 97).

CHAIRS

Some armchairs (box chairs, which England were referred to as 'joyned cheyres') were very similar to contemporary benches with fixed backrests but were narrower and meant for one person. Like benches, they did not have legs but were supported by panelling

[114]
A couple in a French interior. Note the bench in front of the fireplace.

Attributed to Maître François, Valerius Maximus, translated by Simon de Hesdin and Nicholas de Gonesse, *Les Fais et les dis des Romains et de autres gens*, Paris, between 1473 and *c.* 1480; British Library, Harley MS 4375, fol. 42

[115]
Author writing a book. Jean de Meun is sitting on a carved settle that has a curved headboard. Such headboards were typical for fourteenth-century beds, settles and chairs.

Guillaume de Lorris and Jean de Meun, *Roman de la rose*, Paris, *c.* 1380; British Library, Yates Thompson MS 21, fol. 69 v

[116]
Philosophy and Boethius. Philosophy is sitting in an x-framed chair and Boethius is resting on a bed surrounded by hangings. The wall is faced in stone and decorated with architectural medallions. The floor is paved with large stone tiles.

Attributed to Jean Colombe, Boethius, *Le Livre de Boece de consolacion* (anonymous French translation), Book 5, France, Bourges, 1477; British Library, Harley MS 4339, fol. 2

on all four sides. Linenfold carving, which emerged in Flanders about 1450 and was subsequently transferred to other countries (to England *c.* 1500), was a favourite type of decoration for these. Sixteenth-century items could include classical ornament, which in England was called 'Romayne' or 'Anticke'. They were frequently shown in high-status and middle-class Flemish bedrooms and placed just next to the bedstead. Sometimes they were designed, produced and installed *en suite* with other armchairs, benches and beds (Fig. 5, 11).

Rarer and more elaborate seats of this type had a very high curved backrest or a tester and are normally depicted as settles in French or Flemish studies or in formal rooms as seats of honour (Fig. 39, 104, 115). However, the traditional types of seat of honour, used across Europe, were x-framed chairs. Their original construction was relatively complicated, as it was derived from sophisticated and magnificent antique folding chairs. Sometimes they would have a backrest and armrests. They could be of cast metal (like the iconic Dagobert's chair), but more frequently they were made of wood, and often richly decorated (Fig. 15, 16, 56, 107, 116, 131, 132).

Modest folding chairs shared the same ancestors as x-framed chairs, but were their very poor relations. Made of plain wood and utilitarian, they were very popular in northern Europe throughout the Middle Ages and the Renaissance. In fifteenth- and sixteenth-century Flanders some of these would have a primitive backrest consisting of an upright with a horizontal board. Such chairs can frequently be seen in illustrations of

peasant and artisan interiors, though some might also come from higher-status settings (Fig. 51, 118).

In Italy, the most popular type of chair with all classes was a rustic chair with a ladder back and a seat made of rushes. In use for centuries, it came in many variations (Fig. 73, 80). Its northern European cousin, made of bentwood, can be seen in the masterly illumination from the Hours of Catherine of Cleves (Fig. 72). The same miniature shows another typically northern European type of rustic seat: a barrel-shaped armchair, one of the favourites in fifteenth- and sixteenth-century Flemish illuminations of artisan and middle-class interiors (Fig. 67). Possibly related to barrel-chairs were short, cylindrical armchairs. They were shown in fifteenth-century French miniatures, frequently next to beds in wealthy interiors (Fig. 91, 104).

STOOLS

Stools were the most popular type of seating furniture and all European households had them (Fig. 7, 51, 97, 117, 140). They differed in quality and the most primitive ones would look like a typical milking stool and consist of a seat and three rough-hewn legs. The less basic stools had four legs, which could be turned on a lathe. In fifteenth-century Italy

[117]
The Last Supper, set at a round table in the loggia of a country estate. Note the chairs and stools typical for Flanders.

Attributed to the workshop of the Master of James IV of Scotland, Book of Hours (Hours of Joanna I of Castile), Flanders (Ghent?), c. 1500; British Library, Add. MS 35313, fol. 19

[118]
St Mark copying a manuscript. The study is dominated by an elaborately designed x-framed chair, a symbol of distinction. The barrel ceiling is panelled with wood and decorated with metal bosses.

Simon Marmion and workshop, cuttings from a Book of Hours, France (Valenciennes), late 1460s; British Library, Add. MS 71117, fol. D

stools often had sides that tapered upwards. This type of box-like, patrician, stool had a large surface that was used for decoration: painting, *tarsie* or carving. Their northern European contemporary equivalents had straight side panels, which were cut out in decorative Gothic patterns to create a lighter and more elegant piece of furniture that could be moved about more easily.

7. Tables

TRESTLE TABLES

The simplest, most popular and characteristic medieval and Renaissance table consisted of a wooden board and two detachable sets of trestles. This form probably originated in Spain: in England they were called 'Spanish tables' and Italian inventories described their trestles as legs '*alla spagnola*' (Fig. 119).

Most trestle tables were long and narrow and were supported by a pair of trestles at each end of the table-top. The upper parts of the table legs had to be hinged to the under-side of the board to keep them in place. Many trestles were also braced with metal hooks. The trestles had three legs each and were positioned under the table in such a way as to minimise disturbance to the diners. This was easily done because the diners normally sat only at the head and on one side of the table, not opposite each other (Fig. 120). The single legs of the trestles were therefore often positioned on the occupied side of table, so there was less in the diners' way, and the two remaining sturdier legs of each trestle, which were set in an upside-down 'v' and often braced, were placed at the front of the

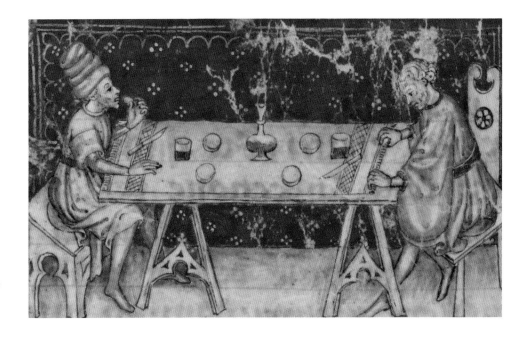

[119]
Men at a trestle table. Two men seated at a Gothic trestle table laid with a tablecloth. The joined stool and the high-backed chair with stacked legs are also Gothic in design. The wine decanter and glass tumblers are not a luxury: they were commonplace in fifteenth-century Italy.

Flore de virtu e de costumi (Flowers of Virtue and of Custom), Padua?, second quarter of the 15th century; British Library, Harley MS 3448, fol. 2 v

[120]
Sir Geoffrey Luttrell sitting at a trestle table with his family.

Psalter (Luttrell Psalter), England (Lincoln), 1325–40; British Library, Add. MS 42130, fol. 208

table, where nobody was sitting. As the front part of the trestles was the only surface of the table visible to the onlooker, it was often fashionably decorated (Fig. 84, 119).

Trestle table-tops could also be decorated to some degree, but being moved very often they must have been prone to damage and therefore most of the time they were kept plain, which also made them easy to clean. Most tables were covered with white table cloths before meals. According to one's means and status, tablecloths could be made either of very valuable damask or of cheaper linen. The quality of tablecloth linen varied and it could be embellished with woven ornamental bands and other decorative patterns, which were usually dyed blue. Depending on the region and fashion, such tablecloth decoration could come in other colours, such as black or red. Tassels were also a very popular way of decorating tablecloths (Fig. 119).

Trestle tables were used in all households, from the royal and princely to the humblest and poorest, though the quality of the craftsmanship, the size of the tables and the type of wood used to make them would vary. The majority of such tables for use by a large number of diners had narrow rectangular table-tops. Some trestle tables were round, though these were frequently much smaller, supported by one trestle and meant for use by one or two diners.

Trestle tables were very popular and remained in use for many centuries because they could be set up before meals and dismantled and stowed away out of sight afterwards. Such tables are generally depicted in front of fireplaces (Fig. 121). The best illustrations of such arrangements in France and Flanders are calendar illuminations for the winter months showing how trestle tables were used in the richest households. The illuminations for the month of January from the Grimani Breviary and the Très Riches Heures of the Duc de Berrry are the best examples of this practice among the ruling elite to be found in illuminated manuscripts (Fig. 125, 126).

Setting up a table in front of the fireplace was especially desirable in cold winter months, when the diners at large receptions would sit on a bench (sometimes with a movable backrest) or on chairs wedged between the table and a roaring fire. Sometimes a wicker or perforated wooden fire-screen was placed between the diners and the fireplace to shield them from excessive heat (Fig. 70, 81, 125, 126).

In the summer, the same trestle tables could easily be moved and used to dine *al fresco*, though a sixteenth-century German illumination from the *Splendor Solis* manuscript shows a garden party at a smallish table that seems to be fitted with integrated legs and braces placed above the ground. The braces are in the form of narrow boards, which can serve as footrests (Fig. 92). The robust-looking tables shown in the illuminations from two Polish manuscripts, the Behem Codex and the *Pontifical of Erazm Ciolek*, were typical for fifteenth- and sixteenth-century interiors in central Europe, mainly in the German-speaking countries of the Habsburg Empire and in Poland (Fig. 58, 98, 112). However, they were also known in southern Europe. Some examples survive in the Palazzo Davanzati in Florence. They are also depicted on historiated Italian maiolica, such as a plate (*tagliere*) made *c.* 1525–30 at Urbino and showing the birth of Hercules taking place in a high-status bedroom (now in the Victoria and Albert Museum). This type of table consisted of a table-top and two supporting boards placed at each table end on the central axis. The supports were joined by stretchers, which were locked in place with bolts. The edges of the supports were decorated with carving.

Such tables are seen in both domestic and institutional settings and must have been very practical and popular in all milieus. This type of table was very strong and stable and it was so popular that the same basic construction was used as a blueprint to produce appropriately modified tables for use in dining halls, bedrooms, workshops and studies. Lucas Cranach's 1526 painting of Cardinal Albrecht of Brandenburg shows that tables of this type used in studies could be totally integrated into their surroundings, making up a matching set with other study furniture.

TABLES WITH FIXED SUPPORTS

Trestle tables gradually went out of fashion in course of the Renaissance, though this useful and space-saving design is still used in the twenty-first century. They were super-seded by tables with fixed supports.

Simple tables, rectangular or round, with stake legs must have been popular for centuries and used by all households. They can be seen in illuminations coming from all over Europe (Fig. 5–7). Essentially, they were constructed in the same way as the simplest of stools for sitting. Both types of furniture, supported by stake legs, must have been very cheap and, depending on the material and quality of the finished product, affordable even by the poorest.

Another type of a table may be depicted in a Flemish illumination showing a country squire at a simple table for one person. Only one very broad table leg (or support) is visible here but such a table could possibly be a late example of a sturdy polyhedral table (Fig. 67). Such tables were fashionable in the Netherlands at the beginning of the fifteenth century. Detailed depictions of them can be seen in paintings by the Master of Flémalle: in the Brussels Annunciation and in the Mérode Altarpiece.

Later on, in the sixteenth century, draw-tables were considered to be typically Netherlandish and French. These had a double layer of extendable table-tops, which could be drawn out when needed in order to increase the usable table surface.

In contrast to the trestle tables in the January scenes of the Grimani and Berry manu-scripts, the early sixteenth-century Flemish illumination for the month of February in the Golf Book illumination shows a sturdy-looking, compact table with fixed braced legs (Fig. 70). Such a small table, fit for two diners only, probably was not stationary. It could have been placed against the wall and moved to another room after the meal. A small dining table like this could hardly have been used on its own and side-tables for carving, pouring drinks and putting food on platters had to be placed beside it. Larger tableware did not fit on the dining table either and was also placed on the side-table. In fact, side- tables were used even alongside very large dining tables and some of them were referred to as buffets, *dressoirs* or *credenza*s.

[121]
Calendar page for January. Feasting. Note the buffet.

Book of Hours, France (Amiens), between 1430 and 1440; British Library, Add. MS 31835, fol. 1 v

BUFFETS

Generally, the three terms buffet, *dressoir* and *credenza* are used interchangeably for similar pieces of northern and southern European furniture, performing similar display and food-preparation functions, though the Italian variant one would usually call a *credenza*. They probably originated in Italy and became very popular in most parts of Europe. The original function of a *credenza* (in high-status households) was the tasting of food and drink to check it was not poisoned, hence the Italian name, which means faith. Many other languages took this name over: credence in English, *Credentz* in German and *kredens* in Dutch and Polish. In French this type of 'table-cum-cupboard' is normally called a *dressoir*, also known in English as a buffet (Fig. 121).

Initially medieval buffets were simple tables. In the fifteenth century they were trans-formed into very broad and tall tiered buffets and later on, in the sixteenth century, especially in northern Europe, into elaborate, lockable cupboards. It is worth noting that in the fifteenth century, Italian *credenzas* tended to be stepped tables without a lockable unit, while in Flanders, closed buffets seemed to be favoured, though some of them could have stepped units on top (Fig. 83, 122, 125, 126). Simple *credenza*s were often covered with a tablecloth or additionally decorated with a wall hanging placed behind them. Lockable buffets were often richly carved and sometimes painted (Fig. 60, 65).

Although *credenza*s initially served as practical side-tables, they were adapted for another purpose and used mainly for the display of prestigious tableware, mostly made

[122]
Tuscan *credenza* with tableware
on display. *Credenzas* consisting of
staged shelves were used to display
tableware, especially during feasts.

The Florentine Picture-Chronicle, Florence,
c. 1470–75; British Museum, London, Prints
& Drawings 1889,0527.77

of polished brass, precious metals, glass, crystal or maiolica. In lockable *credenza*s, valuable tableware and linen could be kept permanently, avoiding the need to put the articles away into secure storage. *Credenza*s were mainly used by royal and princely households, but they also appealed to the lower nobility and were very popular with patricians. The lower classes seem to have had similar, though much more modest, pieces of furniture imitating *credenza*s: these were cupboards in which to display and keep their best possessions. It is worth mentioning that some countries in the fifteenth century observed strict sumptuary or precedence laws regulating the look of tiered *credenza*s. Generally, the higher up the social scale one was, the higher one's *credenza* and the number of tiers allowed.

EN-SUITE AND DECORATIVE TABLES

Decorative carved furniture made *en suite* with a table can be seen in an illumination showing Henry VIII in a loggia with his jester (Fig. 110). The king is sitting at a table – or possibly at a chest? This handsome piece of furniture seems to be *en suite* with the seat next to it and with the king's bed depicted in a separate illumination (Fig. 106). As it is assumed that both illuminations show a fictional palace and its imaginary interiors, it could also be concluded that the table depicted is there just for decoration. It seems unlikely to have been actually used as a table because there is no room for the king's knees, so sitting at it would have been very awkward. However, other equally impractical objects were also shown functioning as tables in other contemporary representations, such as chests of a sarcophagus type. Such chests were very fashionable mainly in Italy around the year 1500, and were closely related to the table depicted in the design of their very curious and grandiose legs, described in Francesco Colonna's 1499 *Hypnero-tomachia Polifili* as 'harpies' legs dressed in foliage'. While the table in Fig. 110 is boxlike and has straight side panels, the *bombé* shape of the side walls of the more flamboyant sarcophagus chests would have made sitting at them even more difficult, and yet two late fifteenth- and early sixteenth-century engravings show a scholar and a poet, respectively, seated at these unwieldy pieces of furniture and using them as tables. This could mean that some chests were indeed adopted for use as tables or desks and that, possibly, some knee space could have been created on the side invisible to the viewer. Maybe these awkward-looking tables were accepted because chests of similar design were very pleasing to the eye and extremely fashionable. Consequently, it would have made sense to match the design of other key pieces of furniture to create a uniformly harmonious and elegant furnishing scheme, even if it had to be done at the expense of comfort. It might be that the added advantage of great storage potential in such a piece of household equipment outweighed the impracticalities, as the table-top must have been hinged and probably lockable, and the inside of the table hollow.

On the other hand, not all fixtures and fittings had to be practical, especially in royal and princely interiors. There are numerous examples of luxurious and purely decorative tables. These were made from expensive materials such as inlaid and carved wood or marble. Many marble table-tops were inlaid with small cut stones to create intricate mosaics. Such extravagant tables, designed almost entirely for show, were very fashionable from the sixteenth century onwards and Italian craftsmen specialised in producing these.

VI
DISPLAY OF WEALTH, IDEAS AND VALUES THROUGH DOMESTIC OBJECTS

Houses were not only the place where basic safety, comforts and privacy could be found. Social elites all over Europe also used them as settings for the display of wealth, power, intellectual ideas and higher values (aesthetic, moral, cultural, religious and political). This was done not only through patronage of architecture and interior decoration but also through appreciation of fine, costly, rare, and technically and artistically advanced objects – whether antique or modern – that conveyed and confirmed the inner virtues and refinement of their owners. Such display could take place anywhere in the house, and publicly accessible halls and studies were the most suitable rooms for this role. By contrast, as already discussed, family values were mainly celebrated through material possessions accumulated in more private spaces, mainly bedrooms. Although relatively small, these objects were often very decorative and, as such, contributed considerably to the overall appearance of interiors. As they were very important to their owners, some of the best illuminations depict them in minute detail.

1. Fine Dining, Luxury Display or Symbol

GOLD AND SILVER TABLEWARE

Medieval and Renaissance metal tableware, plates, bowls, beakers, jugs and other dishes and vessels could be plain utilitarian objects, and the lower classes of society often treated them as such, but they also gave owners and users an opportunity to show off their good taste, sophistication and wealth. One prized not only the materials from which such dishes and vessels were made but also their design and the skill of the craftsmen producing them (Fig. 123, 124).

Members of the highest ranks of society usually had several gold, silver and gilded table services. The basic form of dishes and vessels has not developed much over the centuries but their embellishments have been more susceptible to changes. Depending on fashion, technological advances and the skill and tools of the craftsman, these pieces were often decorated with the usual metalwork techniques, chasing, embossing and enamelling being the favourite for these types of objects. Gemstones were also used to embellish some tableware, though gem-encrusted objects were normally meant to be

[123]
The marriage feast at Cana. Wedding guests are seated at a table. Medieval diners would usually sit on simple benches arranged against a wall. The table is laid with pewter or ceramic dishes and vessels, which were shared between guests. Note the lack of individual plates. Many dishes would have been eaten with the fingers. Guests would usually bring their own knives and spoons; forks were very rarely used until the Renaissance.

Herman Scheerre (?), the Bible with the Gospel of Nicodemus and the Interpretation of Hebrew Names, England (London?), first quarter of the 15th century; British Library, Royal MS 1 E IX, fol. 276

[124]
A goldsmith's shop. The luxurious metal tableware would have been displayed at home on a buffet. Other trinkets, such as jewellery and belt buckles, would have been suitable as betrothal presents. Valuables such as these could have been housed in a study, which often provided secure storage.

Lapidaire de Mandeville, Flanders, last quarter of the 15th century; Bibliothèque Nationale de France, Paris, MS Fr. 9136, fol. 344

purely decorative and were put on display as a status statement rather than used at the table like other more modest pieces of a service.

Great quantities of gold and silverware were once owned by the royal and princely households, but only a small number have survived. The value of the precious metal almost always outweighed the artistic value of the goldsmith's highly skilled craftsmanship and most of these objects were melted down in times of war and financial crisis. Some of the goldsmiths' masterpieces were extremely short-lived and did not even survive their makers or their patrons. This often happened when military campaigns had to be funded. It cannot have been easy for the collectors and it must have been very demoralising for the craftsmen. Lorenzo Ghiberti in his *I Commentarii* related a story about one of his fellow goldsmiths, Gusmin of Cologne, who withdrew to a monastery and became a hermit on hearing that Louis I, Duke of Anjou and King of Naples, had had his work melted down and struck into coins to fund a military campaign in 1382.

Because goods made of gold and silver were so often broken up and turned into coins, it was important to regulate the standard of the metal alloys used by goldsmiths and silversmiths. In England this was done by the Goldsmiths' Company, which controlled the workshops. Imposing standards was not always easy or successful. The charter of the Goldsmiths' Company, issued in 1327 by Edward III, stated that the London goldsmiths' workshops had to be set up only in Cheapside, their own quarter. This was mainly to counteract the practice of establishing workshops that were purposely difficult to find and to control. Such workshops could easily avoid supervision and secretly use poor-quality alloys for the production of their goods.

The majority of gold and silverware pieces still extant were donated to religious establishments and were thus spared a cruel fate, but this is only a handful of the ones made. Consequently, most of the information we have about this type of metalware comes from inventories, accounts, memoirs, paintings and illuminations.

Princely and royal patrons often ordered gold and silverwork directly from the goldsmiths. Many precious metal objects were also presented to them by other people of their own rank and by their subjects. New Year was traditionally the best time to give gold and silver objects and tableware was one of the favourite choices for such a present. One such New Year gift recorded was six gold trenchers engraved with the French arms, presented in 1394 to Charles VI of France by the Paris tax collectors. In 1481–2, again at Christmas and New Year, Edward IV of England placed a very considerable order for various pieces of precious metal tableware. The set included cups, bowls, plates, flagons and a salt-cellar. The craftsman entrusted with the work was a London based goldsmith, John Shaa.

The giving of New Year presents was connected with New Year festivities, which often would have included a reception. Many illuminations for the month of January in medieval and Renaissance calendars show winter feasts and festivities. Two of these illuminations are outstanding and provide us with an exceptional glimpse of fine dining and display. The first one is in the Très Riches Heures of the Duc de Berry, and the second is in the Grimani Breviary (Fig. 125, 126).

The Très Riches Heures was commissioned by Jean, Duc de Berry, one of the three younger brothers of King Charles V of France, and produced by the Limbourg brothers' workshop in the years 1411–16. The original illuminators left the manuscript unfinished and it was not until five decades later that work on the manuscript continued. The Grimani Breviary was probably produced between 1510 and 1520 – about a century after the original work on the Très Riches Heures. It was illuminated by several leading Flemish artists and their workshops. No documentary evidence about the origins of the Grimani Breviary is known but stylistic analysis indicates that the contributors included Simon Bening, Gerard David and the Master of James IV of Scotland. Unfortunately, we do not know who commissioned the manuscript or who its first owner was. However, we do know that by 1520, shortly after the work on the manuscript was completed, it was owned by Cardinal Domenico Grimani, and that it has stayed in Venice ever since. We can also reasonably assume that its illuminators must have had access to the finished Très Riches Heures, as some illuminations of the Grimani Breviary are based on the miniatures of the older manuscript, which were partially executed when work started

on the manuscript and finished in the second period of work (in the September Très Riches Heures illumination, for example, the background shows the castle of Saumur painted by the Limbourg workshop and a harvest scene in the foreground added and finished by Jean Colombe several decades later).

The January scenes reproduced here were executed about a century apart from each other, but it is clear at first glance that the composition of the later illumination must have been based on the Limbourgs' original. The layout of the rooms depicted is similar, as is the positioning of the main protagonists, but all the details of the interior represented in the Grimani January scene are updated and rendered with greater precision than those in the matching Berry folio. The Grimani Breviary is bigger than the Très Riches Heures, which made the illuminator's work easier; nevertheless, the the realism achieved here is truly remarkable and masterly. For comparison, and to appreciate the achievements of the Limbourgs and those of the Grimani illuminator, a useful comparison can be made with a third January illumination, based on the Très Riches Heures January folio, in the Dunois Hours, now in the British Library (Fig. 71). The dimensions of this illumination are very small, and the miniature is not in the best condition, but even taking those adverse circumstances into account, a more skilled illuminator such as the one of the Grimani Breviary, or possibly the Limbourgs, would have been able to depict details with more precision. The Dunois Hours was made in Paris by an associate of the Master of the Bedford Hours whose name is unknown. They were produced in about 1440–50 and commissioned by (or for) Jean, Comte de Dunois, Bastard of Orleans, whose sketchy portrait is included in the January miniature and who is identifiable by his arms (modified fleurs-de-lis) on the wall hanging and on the chimneypiece. (There are also nineteen other folios in this manuscript decorated with his heraldry and with two other portraits of him.) All three of these January illuminations, although very similar in composition, show variations in the dishes and vessels depicted, and these reflect typological changes in fashion.

While all dishes and vessels used by royalty, the nobility and the highest ranks of the clergy were important for practical reasons, one of them, a *nef*, was an *objet d'art* serving more as a status symbol than as a useful container. The aptly named *nef* had the form of a ship. Its French name was used in other countries as well. The oldest archival document mentioning a silver-gilt *nef* dates back to 1239. *Nefs* were normally placed on the table in front of or next to the head of the household, or the most important person at the reception. The ones which served as an indication of the diner's status would normally be the biggest object or vessel on the table and it is probably for this reason that they were sometimes fitted with wheels. Olivier de La Marche – a Burgundian court official of Philip the Good and Charles the Bold – noted in his *Mémoires* of 1474 that the *nefs* of the Burgundian dukes were so big that they could not be placed in front of them because ambassadors or princes wishing to speak to the dukes would not be able to see them. Instead, the big *nefs* had to be placed out of the way, at the head of the table.

[125]
Calendar page for January. The Duc de Berry feasting with his household and courtiers.

Limbourg brothers' workshop, Les Très Riches Heures de Jean de France, Duc de Berry, Franco-Netherlandish, Limbourg brothers active in France, 1411/12–16; Musée Condé, Chantilly, MS 65, fol. 1 v

All three miniatures also show large *nefs*, displayed in the same fashion, at the head of the table. However, *nefs* were not always very big. Charles V of France, Jean de Berry's elder brother, owned many *nefs* made of gold and silver and of varying sizes, both large and small (the small ones were called *navettes*). While gold and silver were the usual material from which *nefs* were made, sometimes the bowl of the vessel was made of a different material, such as semi-precious stone. One surviving example is made of cornelian and of parcel-gilded and enamelled silver. It was produced in a Tours workshop, is now housed at Reims cathedral and serves as a reliquary of St Ursula.

The practical function of a *nef* was as a container for personal table utensils (mainly cutlery and crockery). The *nef* shown next to Jean de Berry seems to contain plates (or trenchers). The small vessel next to it is probably a salt-cellar, which often would also be kept in the *nef* and could take the form of a little ship (*navette*). Inventories indicate that Charles V of France owned such salt-cellars. He also owned a personal silver-gilded *nef* in which he held his personal plates and cutlery: a knife, spoon and aork. It is worth mentioning at this point that forks were an absolute novelty and a luxury at a medieval table. No illumination shows a fork and this is no coincidence: depictions of early forks are very rare, which no doubt reflects the rarity of forks at that time. The earliest recorded forks were owned by the highest circles of society in France and Italy in the fourteenth and fifteenth centuries. It is assumed that initially they were used for sweetmeats. Gradually this piece of cutlery turned out to be useful for many other dishes as well. It became widely spread all over Europe and fashionable among all classes and used together with knives and spoons. Cutlery was frequently considered to be very personal, and many people – including sometimes the nobility – used to carry their own cutlery with them, even when invited to banquets. Curiously, this custom survived after the Renaissance. These personal sets of cutlery were often very decorative and kept in equally presentable *cuir boulli* cases designed and made especially for the purpose. Fragile and valuable drinking cups or personal travel goblets could be kept in similar cases, which where additionally padded and lined on the inside. In this way they fitted tightly around the vessels and protected them from damage. Such a case would have been needed for the glass cup which stands in front of the diner in the Grimani Breviary illumination. The cup has a fluted pattern on the bowl and the lid. The finial of the lid, the rims of the lid and the cup, the foot of the cup and its central boss are all decorated with gold settings. This type of cup could also have been set with precious stones or pearls and decorated with enamel. The cups on the Duc de Berry's January reception table are of an older type than this valuable cup. Such cups were called *hanaps* and were often made of gold or silver, sometimes gilded. Their form was simpler and they were shorter than later cups. Some have wooden bowls, which were not unusual, even in royal circles. Wood was much lighter than metal, and costly woods were used, such as sycamore, beech or aloe. One of the surviving cups of this type is the Royal Gold Cup, now in the British Museum. It was probably commissioned by the Duc de Berry as a present for his brother, Charles

[126]
Calendar page for January in a Flemish interior. Feasting by the fire in a noble household.

Master of James IV of Scotland; Grimani Breviary, Flanders, *c.* 1510–20; Biblioteca Nazionale Marciana, Venice, Italy, cod. Lat. I, 99 (=2138), fol. 1 v

V, in the late fourteenth century, and is made of gold, enamelled with scenes from the life of St Agnes and set with gemstones and pearls. It was originally more lavishly decorated and shorter, but its stem is now quite long as it has been altered twice, made taller probably owing to changing fashion and owners. The two decorative bands, one with Tudor Roses and the other with commemorative inscriptions, were also added later.

The most common form of drinking vessel was a simple bowl with a very shallow foot (or rather a stand-ring). They stayed in use for a very long time, and we can see examples of such bowls set out on depicted tables and stacked on *dressoirs* in the Berry and Grimani manuscripts. They were made of precious metals and often decorated with simple chasing, engraving or enamelled coat of arms on the inside.

The form of the shallower dishes in the January scenes – the trenchers, plates and platters – has survived virtually unchanged. It seems that the dishes in our illuminations were made of gold but the covers (possibly protecting the food from getting cold and guarding it from the dogs sniffing at, or even on, the table) were silver or possibly even pewter.

Tableware was both placed on the table and displayed on the *credenza*. To us, displaying tableware may seem a distasteful form of blowing one's own trumpet, but in the Middle Ages and Renaissance the act of displaying wealth, and equally sometimes of hiding it, had practical purposes and was a survival strategy. By displaying costly objects one was able not only to show sophistication and maybe patronage of goldsmiths, but also to prove financial power and therefore imply actual political influence or the possibility of gaining it. Burgundian dukes took part in this practice and sometimes had to put on show the contents of their treasuries, including their tableware – which could subsequently be melted down – to convince their subjects of their ability to finance a planned war. Regular organisation of lavish feasts, banquets, public festivities and parades served the same reassuring purpose.

Yet even the most influential and popular lords, princes and kings could never be certain of their fate, and the Berry, Dunois and Grimani January scenes all illustrate the original function of a *credenza*: the tasting of food and drink. Stewards had to make sure wine was drinkable but, more importantly, check it was not poisoned. Jugs and flagons were not put directly on the table but on the *credenza*, where drinks were tested. In all three illuminations we can see stewards pouring drinks at *credenzas* into the cups they would then carry over to the diners. Food was also tested here, arranged on platters and prepared to be served at table. Apart from jugs, flagons and platters, vessels for storing rinsing water, tablecloths, dishcloths and napkins were also placed here.

MAIOLICA

Types of Maiolica Objects and Their Function

Arguably one of the best illuminations ever executed in Flanders shows a Nativity scene and the Procession of the Magi set in a decorative wooden display cupboard. Valencian

[127]
Shelves with maiolica and glass. The masterly rendition of this illumination allows recognition of the depicted vessels. Most were probably produced locally but the lusterware maiolica (items with metallic gloss decoration) are apparently Spanish (Valencian) imports. The fashion for maiolica came to Flanders via Italy. Maiolica made in northern Europe was initially produced by Italian potters. All the vessels and their contents carry a symbolic Christian meaning and create a border for miniatures of the Adoration of the Magi and their cavalcade. This illumination is probably based on the contents of a cabinet belonging to a nobleman.

Master of Mary of Burgundy, Book of Hours (Hours of Engelbert of Nassau), Flanders, *c.* 1480–90; Bodleian Library, University of Oxford, MS Douce 219, fol. 145 v and fol. 146

and Netherlandish maiolica and glass vessels – symbols of Mary's purity and virginity – are arranged on the shelves, which seem to have been made to measure. Such pieces of furniture could have been produced for curiosity cabinets or studies of patricians or nobility. They were generally used, like museum show cases, for the storage and display of valuable jewels, art and decorative art objects. Sometimes rare natural specimens were kept in such cupboards as well. As this miniature comes from a book of hours associated with Count Engelbert of Nassau, who was a distinguished member of the Burgundian court, it is highly probable that it depicts a part of a nobleman's cabinet (Fig. 127).

The main type of object shown on display in this miniature is maiolica, which in the fifteenth and sixteenth century was considered to be a high-status material. It is accompanied by plain glass vessels, probably of local production, and therefore affordable to many and widely used by the higher and middle ranks of society. The most valuable and acclaimed medieval and Renaissance glass came from Venetian workshops, which were situated on the Venetian island of Murano. Venetian vessels were praised in the fifteenth century for their enamelled decoration and in the sixteenth century for their crystal-clear glass. While most objects made of earthenware, stone, wood, pewter, glass, wool and linen were cheap and used in homes of all social classes, artefacts made of gold, silver, maiolica, Venetian glass, precious and semi-precious stones, pearls, silk and velvet were mainly status symbols and the domain of royalty, the nobility and, if and when sumptuary laws allowed, of the socially ambitious middle classes or artisans..

Maiolica is tin-glazed earthenware. It was covered with an opaque white (or coloured) tin glaze, fired and decorated with strong pigments before it was fired for the second time. The key colours used in the decoration of maiolica were white, blue, green, purple, brown, yellow and orange. It was appreciated and fashionable throughout late medieval and Renaissance Europe. In the strictest sense, the term maiolica refers to the tin-glazed earthenware produced in Renaissance Italy. However, mainly colloquially, the term is also frequently used as a name for the same type of pottery made elsewhere in Europe around that time. Initially, from the twelfth century, tin-glazed earthenware was produced in Spain. In the fifteenth century, maiolica potteries flourished in Italy and from the end of the fifteenth century maiolica was also manufactured in northern Europe, mainly in the southern Netherlands and in England. The same type of pottery, technically, was made north of the Alps in the seventeenth and in the eighteenth centuries and was called 'Delftware' and 'faïence'.

Maiolica was a popular medium for many types of objects. The most frequent maiolica artefacts were generally described as tableware: it was too costly to be used as kitchen-ware. Many other types of cheaper pottery were used for cooking. Maiolica was expensive mainly because of the price of imported tin (which was added to the lead glaze to make it milky white and opaque). Some of the production processes were risky, and results were uncertain, for instance in the production of the ruby-red lustre decoration for which the pottery at Gubbio was famous.

The majority of the surviving maiolica artefacts are dishes, plates, bowls and jugs. All of these were closely associated with the development of the etiquette of fine dining and with the traditional display of wealth in the domestic setting. This custom escalated and spread to all wealthy classes in the late Middle Ages and the Renaissance. The idea was to make a favourable impression on distinguished guests and, in the case of socially ambitious individuals and families, to improve their standing and status. In the case of the latter group this was achieved through conspicuous consumption and spending on objects that showed their owners' sophistication and discerning taste.

Other types of maiolica objects, such as candleholders, small sculptures, mirror frames, inkwells and pen-cases, were also very popular. These were often to be found in studies, which sometimes doubled as treasuries and curiosity cabinets. Floors, walls and sometimes even ceilings could be embellished with maiolica tiles, especially in studies and other parts of domestic interiors intended to show off the wealth and status of the inhabitants. Studies were frequently and typically a male domain. Women, who usually spent most of their free time sewing and spinning, appreciated luxury maiolica spindle-whorls and needle-cases.

Apart from purely domestic use, maiolica technology was also applied in the production of vessels for apothecaries. These were mainly *albarelli*, though this form of a jar could also be found at home, often serving as a container for products bought at a pharmacy (Fig. 127, lower right-hand corner). However, drug jars could be re-purposed and at home some were given a new lease of life and a new function as decorative objects. Other *albarelli* were never meant to serve as drug jars and, like other types of maiolica vessels, were produced as commemorative artefacts from the very start. They might be ordered as betrothal presents and decorated with portraits of the bride and bridegroom, their coats of arms, amorous inscriptions and love emblems.

Maiolica artefacts were much treasured and were displayed in the house. Maiolica tableware would normally have been kept on a *credenza*, usually in a *sala*, a room where the family would gather and receive visitors. Commemorative plates used, like *albarelli* and other objects, to celebrate family events – betrothals, marriages or the arrival of children – could be hung on walls like paintings. These could either decorate the *sala*, or, more probably, one of the more private rooms, such as the marital bedroom. Even the outside of the house could become an appropriate place for showing off one's valued possessions: maiolica vases served as plant pots for evergreens cultivated by the ladies of the house and used to decorate window-sills and loggias.

Maiolica objects not only came in all sorts of shapes and sizes, they were also decorated in many ways and each type of decoration can usually be attributed to a different production centre. Obviously such decoration never stayed exactly the same and we can trace the development of decoration styles over sometimes many decades in which the manufacturers were active.

MAIOLICA AS A CHRISTIAN SYMBOL

Maiolica was so universally admired for its form, design and decoration, and for the technical skill needed to produce it, that all types of maiolica containers – pitchers, jugs, jars and bottles – frequently served as flower vases, though whether or not this was the container's primary function is sometimes unclear. Most such containers are repeatedly depicted in domestic settings, functioning as purely decorative objects in their own right, proudly displayed and often filled with flowers.

An important aspect of maiolica vessels was their depiction in Annunciation scenes, both in panel paintings and in illuminated manuscripts. In this context, the white glaze of maiolica and the preciousness of the material itself stand for the purity of Virgin Mary. The flowers in the vase, most frequently white lilies, reinforce the same symbolic meaning. For instance, two of the earliest representations of maiolica in Netherlandish art can be seen in works by the Master of Flémalle (the Brussels Annunciation of *c.* 1415–25 and the Mérode Altarpiece of *c.* 1427–32).

A much later example of a panel painting showing a maiolica and a glass vessel filled with symbolic flowers is the Portinari Triptych, now in the Uffizi, Florence. It was painted in the late 1470s in Bruges by Hugo van der Goes, whose patron was Tomasso Portinari of the Bruges branch of the Medici bank. Slightly confusingly, in this painting the maiolica – a Valencian lusterware *albarello* – and a glass goblet are shown on the central panel of the triptych, which is devoted to the Adoration of the shepherds. However, this panel is flanked by two wings, which, when closed, expose an Annunciation scene on their reverse. The glass goblet has been added here to reinforce the symbolic meaning; moreover, the lilies in this painting are supplemented by other types of cut flowers, which in turn are carriers of their own Christian messages. In the masterly realism of late medieval Flemish painting, the vessels not only carry the symbolic meaning, but for a devout medieval Christian would have had the power to make the religious experience more immediate and intense: these objects belonged to the material culture of the patron and his contemporaries so that, being painted at eye-level for the viewer and yet on another plane by their inclusion in the religious image, they create an immediate link between the Nativity scene and the material world of the viewer.

The symbolism we find in panel paintings was replicated in illuminated manuscripts. Many illuminations simply repeat the formula of a white glazed maiolica vessel filled with lilies (Fig. 11). However, the two illuminated folios from the book of hours of Engelbert of Nassau develop the imagery further. The manuscript is dated *c.* 1480–90 and the illuminator, referred to as the Master of Mary of Burgundy, not only worked in the same region but also belonged to the same artistic circle as the Master of Flémalle and Hugo van der Goes. As in the Portinari Triptych, the maiolica and the glass vessels are consummately and realistically depicted in the foreground, which belongs to the sphere of the viewers' reality and which in the manuscript provides a very opulent border for the religious events in the illumination. The objects are placed on elaborate shelves either of a study or of a curiosity cabinet and enclose the central illuminations and the text of the Hours of the Virgin. The three green-tinged glass vessels in the illumination (two drinking glasses and a pitcher) could be of local design and production and as such not status indicators but direct Marian symbols. However, the maiolica objects are here more prominent than ever before and take up more space in the miniature than the central religious narrative, which is dominated by the illusionistic border filled with symbolic objects.

MAIOLICA OR GLASS?

Particularly intriguing is one of the vessels shown in the lower left-hand corner of the illumination on fol. 145v. in the book of hours of Engelbert of Nassau (Fig. 127). It appears to be a maiolica bottle. However, when one compares it to a very rare *lattimo* glass flask in the British Museum, it seems likely that the illumination could in fact depict a glass bottle of the same type. Such a conclusion is particularly tempting, as the context of the illumination does show maiolica and glass objects displayed together. The British Museum flask is attributed to Giovanni Maria Obizzo, an enamel painter probably working in Murano, in Venice, and is dated *c.* 1504–9. It is made of milky glass, developed in Venice to imitate Chinese porcelain, which was imported to Europe via Venice. This type of 'faux porcelain' was produced only in Murano and the technology did not spread to any other glass production centre. It is therefore quite safe to assume that the British Museum *lattimo* bottle is of Venetian origin. The form of the bottle, however, seems not to be Italian, but is in fact considered to be northern European, as many Netherlandish tin-glazed earthenware and green-and-blue glass bottles of the same shape have been excavated in England and the Netherlands. We should probably draw the conclusion that the form of the British Museum *lattimo* glass bottle was chosen as a compliment to the English king, Henry VII, for whom it was made. Furthermore, some other Netherlandish tin-glazed earthenware archaeological finds show the same 'IHS' decoration as the one depicted on the vessel from the book of hours of Engelbert of Nassau. For those reasons, and in spite of the interesting parallel, the illumination is highly likely not to show a rare *lattimo* glass bottle. Instead, it almost certainly depicts locally produced Netherlandish tin-glazed earthenware. If this is the case, the miniature's message is more multi-layered than is visible at first glance: it also seems to celebrate a new technological development in the production of pottery used to display both Christian values and sophistication in interior decoration.

2. Studies or 'Treasuries'

STUDIES AND BEGINNINGS OF LIBRARIES, CURIOSITY CABINETS AND MUSEUMS

Many studies, especially those owned by erudite people of considerable wealth and social ambition, doubled as curiosity cabinets and therefore private 'treasuries'. For instance, as we learn from contemporary inventories, documents and eye-witness reports, the study of Piero de' Medici, in the Florentine Palazzo Medici on the Via Larga, mainly housed his collection of vases, jewels, gems, coins and books (Fig. 14). The bindings of the books were ingeniously colour-coded: blue for religion, yellow for grammar, red for poetry and green for art. Although we do not know how Piero de' Medici's collection was stored, one can assume that it was probably kept in inlaid, wooden wall cupboards similar to the ones in Federico da Montefeltro's *studioli* in Urbino and Gubbio. As the Medici study's dimensions were only 4m x 5.5m, the books were probably stored in wall cupboards as well, as the library collection was extensive, and using lecterns to accommodate them would have required a considerably larger room. The Medici inventories do not mention free-standing cupboards, so these must have been built in and integrated

[128]
Contents of a curiosity cabinet or cupboard in a study.

Master of the David scenes in the Grimani Breviary and workshop, Book of Hours (Hours of Joanna I of Castile), Flanders (Bruges or Ghent), between 1496 and 1506; British Library, Add. MS 18852, fol. 40

[129]
Suffrages of Saints, St Mary Magdalene. The jewels in the illusionistic border of this miniature are likely to have been kept in a study.

Workshop of the Maximilian Master, Book of Hours (Hours of Joanna I of Castile), Flanders (Ghent), c. 1500; British Library, Add. MS 35313, fol. 231 v and 232

[130]
St Gregory the Great in his Renaissance study. This study must have been designed as a whole. The furniture is fitted snugly into the tiny space and uniformly decorated.

Giovan Pietro Birago, Book of Hours (Hours of Bona Sforza), Milan, c. 1490–4; British Library, Add. MS 34294, fol. 196 v

into the architectural shell of the study. The interior decoration of this little room intensified the impression of a very well-designed, even if extremely compact, ornate interior as both its floor and its barrel-vaulted ceiling were covered in expensive maiolica tiles. Some of Luca della Robbia's beautifully crafted ceiling tiles for the Medici *studiolo*, depicting signs of the zodiac and labours of the months survive in the collection of the Victoria and Albert Museum.

A handful of remarkable late fifteenth- and early sixteenth-century Flemish manuscript illuminations show cupboards filled with precious items and probably located in studies which, like the *studioli* in Gubbio, Urbino and the Medici palace, were used as a cross between a study and a curiosity cabinet (Fig. 127, 128). Such cupboards seem to act as display cases to put on show an array of precious, beautiful, interesting and symbolic objects: maiolica, metal tableware (probably silver), jewellery, books (probably illuminated manuscripts), natural-history specimens and pictures, which sometimes look like panel paintings fitted snugly between shelves. A couple of these full-page miniatures resemble in composition and content numerous contemporary, and likewise very well-executed Flemish illuminated manuscript borders filled with jewellery, mainly devotional (Fig. 129). It is likely that jewellery was not only kept under lock and key but possibly even exhibited in studies, which in such cases would have a dual function: both curiosity cabinet and strongbox. Some studies were very secure and not easily accessible. The Medici study was, in a way, a walk-in safe and did not have any windows, not even to the well-protected internal courtyard. It is also possible that the jewelled borders of an illuminated manuscript could function as a substitute for a collection of real jewellery or even as potential designs for it. Painted with astonishing illusionism, they certainly had a very strong visual impact. European artisans were sometimes trained in several trades and it has been recorded that the most talented Flemish illuminators and their family members, probably also working in illuminators' workshops, could also be goldsmiths and merchants. Therefore, it is very likely that illuminated borders made use of genuine and contemporary jewellery designs and perhaps provided ideas for commissioning new jewellery.

Some studies also housed collections of arms and armour. Cosimo de' Medici's original Florentine house, predating the palace that was built nearby in the mid-fifteenth century, had an armoury located just behind the study. Famous perspective intarsia panels from Federico da Montefeltro's *studiolo* constructed *c.* 1478–82 at his ducal palace in Gubbio show half-opened wall cupboards filled with several pieces of armour. A sixteenth-century French illumination showing Flavius Josephus in his study illustrates this practice as well (Paris, Bibliothèque Mazarine, MS. 1581, fol. 1).

[131]
Christine de Pizan in her study. Not many women had their own study: such a room was a male domain. Christine was a rare exception: a well-educated widow with access to the royal library, she decided to earn her living by writing. She is shown in her study sitting in a comfortable, upholstered x-framed chair. The floor is tiled with light-coloured tiles, possibly Spanish *cuenca*. The hooks in the wall seem to indicate that the wall hanging is probably real and not just painted. The window is fully glazed, a luxury in 1400.
Attributed to the Master of the Cité des Dames and workshop and to the Master of the Duke of Bedford, Christine de Pizan, various works (the Book of the Queen), Paris, *c.* 1410–*c.* 1414; British Library, Harley MS 4431, fol. 4

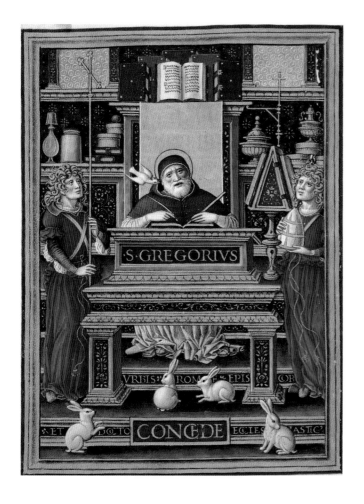

[132]
St Matthew in his 'study' sitting on an x-framed Romanesque chair. The desk and lectern provide support for a scroll.

Attributed to Kokkinobaphos Master; Gospels, evangelists' portraits, Eastern Mediterranean (Constantinople), second quarter of the 12th century; British Library, Burney MS 19, fol. 1 v

[133]
A hermit sitting in a chair with an attached writing board.

Estoire del Saint Graal, La Queste del Saint Graal, Morte Artu, France (Saint-Omer or Tournai?), first quarter of the 14th century; British Library, Royal MS 14 E III, fol. 6 v

STUDY AND LIBRARY FURNITURE

Although not all studies contained objects of high material value (though they usually housed books, which could be extremely expensive), they were often symbols of prestige, social standing and erudition. They usually housed family or business documents, but they also expressed the individuality and values of their owners. Many studies were used as personal space not only for work but also for relaxation. To fulfil their purpose successfully, they had to be well designed and adequately equipped (Fig. 130, 131).

Desks, the principal piece of study furniture, were essentially tables, benches, chests, cupboards or even parts of chairs adapted for reading and writing. Their sometimes complicated and ingenious design goes back to Antiquity. Design details, the types of timber used, and style and decoration may have changed over the ages and followed the general fashion in furniture, but there was little change in the way they were used. Earlier desks had to cater for working on scrolls to a much greater extent than their successors, which were mainly intended to provide a good support for bound books or for rectangular sheets of parchment or paper (Fig. 132). Such a support was best given by boards fixed at an angle to a chair (Fig. 18, 57, 133), free-standing lecterns (Fig. 33, 37, 88, 104, 113, 135) and reading or writing slopes (Fig. 43, 94, 118, 134).

Lecterns came in many shapes and sizes and ranged from a simple support to revolving multifaceted marvels of engineering (Fig. 135). Large movable lecterns were a necessity especially in studies in which scholars used sometimes very large and heavy books. Home study lecterns were mostly designed for seated readers or writers. They were movable in many directions, vertical as well as horizontal, and could be lowered or raised to the desired height by means of adjustable rotating metal or wooden arms.

Many complicated lecterns of this type were used in studies that were sometimes fitted with *en-suite* furniture combining desks and chairs or other seats with built-in cupboards or shelves. Study furniture comprising all these elements normally came as separate components, but some sets were constructed from the outset to form one enormous timber unit (Fig. 136). An unusual example of such a free-standing entity can be seen in Antonello da Messina's *St Jerome in his Study*, now in the National Gallery, London. In manuscript illuminations, especially those depicting Italian Renaissance studies, these kinds of *en-suite* units are generally shown built into a small, almost niche-like room (Fig. 44, 130), though sometimes they are situated in a corner of a larger room, where, like a walk-in cupboard, they were very functional and space saving.

A simple variation on a lectern was a detached reading slope consisting of a main reading surface and two side walls fixed at a desired angle. Sometimes a third board and a bottom panel were added to close the unit, creating a wedge-shaped box. These often had hinged lids, so that one could use them not only as a book support but also as a storage space for small utensils or valuables (Fig. 44, 87, 107).

Both low reading slopes and tall lecterns designed for standing readers were installed not only in private studies but also in public buildings, both secular and ecclesiastical.

In depictions of churches or private chapels at castles or palaces, we see reading slopes located at the altar. Tall lecterns were mostly made for libraries and churches. In a church or a home chapel, they could support the books needed by the priest or by the choir, whose members gathered around a shared copy of a music manuscript. Courts, depending on their type and where they were based, could also use a variation of study furniture.

As manuscripts and early printed books were normally stored horizontally or flat at an angle, medieval and Renaissance libraries used specially adapted lecterns that could also serve as shelving units. This definitely was not a very space-saving solution, but it was practical in the Middle Ages, since most early libraries, especially those for public use, did not have many books. Library books could be placed flat and side by side on such long, bench-like lecterns. Until the invention of print, books were very expensive commodities and were chained to lecterns. This obviously had many disadvantages. The first Oxford University Library had to be replaced by a new library because it ran out of lectern space. The old library's books were apparently packed so tightly on the lecterns that if one reader opened a book it was impossible to read up to four of the books chained next to it. Construction work on the new library, Duke Humfrey's Library, which is now the oldest reading room of the Bodleian Library, was finished in 1488. It was furnished with traditional medieval lecterns instead of book presses, which became fashionable about a century later. The first lecterns in Duke Humfrey's Library were similar in overall design to the library lecterns depicted in two of the British Library's manuscripts: a fourteenth-century illumination from Lydgate's *Pilgrimage of the Life of Man* and a fifteenth-century French illumination from Boethius (Fig. 40, 59).

[134]
Vincent of Beauvais in his study. Note the architectural frame of the miniature and the slanting bookshelves with curtains.

Master of the White Inscriptions, Vincent of Beauvais, *Le Miroir historial* (*Speculum historiale*, trans. into French by Jean de Vignay), Book 1, Bruges, *c.* 1479–*c.* 1480; British Library, Royal MS 14 E I, fol. 3

[135]
St John in his study. Note the revolving lectern with Gothic ornamentation, the glazed window, the desk chair, typically French in form, and the folding stool (seen often in Flanders as well as in France).

The Bedford Master, Book of Hours (The Bedford Hours), Paris, *c.* 1423–30; British Library, Add. MS 18850, fol. 19

[136]
Author writing a book. The walls of the study are faced with stone or decorated with imitation stone. The floor is paved with green glazed tiles. The splayed windows are permanently glazed. Note the comfortably designed small desk unit. The wooden platform keeps the author's feet warm and away from the cold floor.

Master of the Prayer Books of around 1500, Guillaume de Lorris and Jean de Meun, *Roman de la rose*, Bruges, *c.* 1490–*c.* 1500; British Library, Harley MS 4425, fol. 133

BOOKS AND THEIR STORAGE

Generally, in a home study, it made more sense for lecterns to be combined with desks and other furniture in order to store books, stationery and other study equipment. Depending on how many books one had, these could be stored either directly on a lectern or a desk, or on tables or cupboards of various shapes underneath them. Cupboards with multiple shelves could also line study walls, and could have lockable doors (Fig. 137). Books could also be kept in chests, which were locked, if needed, and sometimes used as seats (Fig. 43). Obviously, shelves fixed to the walls existed as well. Books were arranged on them either horizontally, or upright with their front or back covers exposed as on a lectern. For several reasons, this was more practical than shelving them cover to cover, with spines exposed, the way we do it today. First, early books were often very large and would have become deformed if shelved on their lower edge. Second, they often had large metal bosses in the centre and on the edges of the covers. Third, they also had protruding metal fasteners and clasps, which were necessary to keep bindings closed but made it impossible to arrange a library in a modern way. The metal embellishments on books were frequently very decorative but they were mainly functional. As parchment pages tend to roll up, forcing the book to open, they were needed to keep books closed to protect them from dust, humidity, light and pests. Such protection from the environment was also an additional reason to keep books in chests and cupboards. With a growing number of books, storage in chests or on lecterns started to be awkward and books were arranged on shelves. This potentially exposed them to damage; one way of guarding against this was to hang curtains in front of them (Fig. 134).

STATIONERY, UTENSILS AND INSTRUMENTS

Apart from desks, lecterns, cupboards, chests, shelves and books, one needed quite a lot of stationery and other equipment. The usual items to be found in studies can be seen nicely arranged in a 1525 Venice print from Giovanantonio Tagliente's *'La vera arte dello excellente scrivere'* (Fig. 138). The items shown here are those owned by a calligrapher, but most of them are also seen depicted in studies used by scholars: books, quill pens, pen-knives for preparing quills and for erasing mistakes from parchment, inkwells, ink-bottles, containers for sand, oil lamps, candles in candleholders, hourglasses, seals, scissors, rulers, set-squares, compasses and twine. Sometimes such ensembles could be complemented by all sorts of lead weights on cords for keeping the pages of books open,

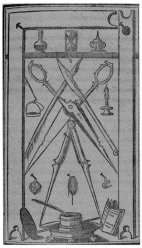

[137]
St Luke seated at an easel in his study and painting the Virgin Mary. The study is furnished with a splendid bookcase consisting of shelves and cupboards with doors. Luxuriously bound books are arranged in a medieval fashion, with their front covers exposed. As St Luke was a scholar, painter and physician, the vessels on the top shelves probably contain ink, pigments and medicine. The large casement windows are glazed with good-quality clear glass in order to let in plenty of natural light. The coffered ceiling is Renaissance in style but a Gothic-style bedchamber is visible in the background.

Master of the David Scenes in the Grimani Breviary; Book of Hours, Flanders, beginning of the 16th century; Bodleian Library, University of Oxford, MS Douce 112, fol. 23 v

[138]
Writing utensils and study equipment. Such objects were stored out of sight in desks, displayed on shelves or hung either on walls or on pieces of furniture in studies.

G. A. Tagliente, *La vera arte dello excellente scrivere*, Venice, 1525; British Library C.31 f.15

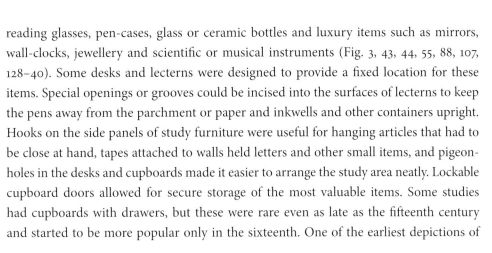

reading glasses, pen-cases, glass or ceramic bottles and luxury items such as mirrors, wall-clocks, jewellery and scientific or musical instruments (Fig. 3, 43, 44, 55, 88, 107, 128–40). Some desks and lecterns were designed to provide a fixed location for these items. Special openings or grooves could be incised into the surfaces of lecterns to keep the pens away from the parchment or paper and inkwells and other containers upright. Hooks on the side panels of study furniture were useful for hanging articles that had to be close at hand, tapes attached to walls held letters and other small items, and pigeon-holes in the desks and cupboards made it easier to arrange the study area neatly. Lockable cupboard doors allowed for secure storage of the most valuable items. Some studies had cupboards with drawers, but these were rare even as late as the fifteenth century and started to be more popular only in the sixteenth. One of the earliest depictions of

[139]
A study housing books and musical instruments, with musicians playing. Musical instruments were often kept in studies.

Attributed to Maître François, Valerius Maximus, translated by Simon de Hesdin and Nicholas de Gonesse, *Les Fais et les dis des Romains et de autres gens*, Paris, between 1473 and c. 1480; British Library, Harley MS 4375, fol. 151 v

drawers can be seen in the Ognissanti church in Florence in Botticelli's 1480 fresco of St Augustine's study.

ILLUMINATORS' WORKSHOPS

Archival sources indicate that not only scholars and scribes had studies; people from other walks of life, especially merchants and bankers, also had such rooms, which they used mainly for business correspondence and accounts. Illuminators also owned studies, furnished and equipped as befitted their work, and some of these are shown in miniatures of St Luke at work painting the Virgin (Fig. 61, 137, 140).

Artists often replicated such images to include their self-portraits in paintings and represent themselves as St Luke, the patron of their guild. Simon Bening, one of the last leading sixteenth-century Flemish illuminators, depicted himself in this fashion in his two self-portraits of 1558. In Bening's study in Bruges, the painter is sitting at an easel next to a glazed window and working on a miniature of the Virgin Mary. The artist is shown holding a pair of spectacles, which seems to confirm that he must have used magnification to produce some of his exquisite illuminations. It is unlikely that the minute realistic details of many works of art depicting the late medieval and Renaissance

[140]
St Luke at an easel painting the Virgin in a Flemish artisan interior. Illuminators' workshops are often represented as a hybrid of a painter's workshop and a study. Note the *lavabo* niche at the door, jars with pigments on the shelves, a wall cupboard, the typically Flemish stools, and especially a stool with a backrest such as would usually furnish a poorer household. This illumination is very small (42.5 x 42.5 mm), so here it has been enlarged to show the minute details, probably executed using a magnifying glass.

Book of Hours, Flanders, *c.* 1510; Fitzwilliam Museum, University of Cambridge, MS 1058–1975, fol. 36

world could have been executed, with sometimes astonishing precision, without the aid of strong magnifying glasses, and numerous illuminations reproduced in this publication bear witness to this practice.

Although artistic licence has to be allowed to illuminators and caution is advised before interpreting their work at face value, miniatures, just like other works of art, can be appreciated and prove a valuable resource for the study of interiors when considered in the wider socio-economic, intellectual, religious, political, cultural and artistic context of the fascinating times in which they were created. Bearing these complex issues in mind, this book has attempted to give a brief and general introduction to various aspects of medieval and Renaissance interiors and, when possible, to show how these were reflected in illuminations.

Further Reading

Most of the institutions mentioned in the text, especially libraries, museums and galleries, have digital databases of images and online catalogues of their collections.

M. Ajmar-Wohlheim and F. Dennis (eds), *At Home in Renaissance Italy* (London: V&A Publications; New York: Abrams, 2006)

J. J. G. Alexander, *Medieval Illuminators and their Methods of Work* (New Haven, London: Yale University Press, 1992)

J. Backhouse, *The Illuminated Manuscript* (Oxford: Phaidon, 1979)

P. Basing, *Trades and Crafts in Medieval Manuscripts* (London: British Library, 1979)

A. Bayer (ed.), *Art and Love in Renaissance Italy* (New York: Metropolitan Museum of Art; New York: Harry N. Abrams, 2008)

P. Binski, *Painters* (London: British Museum Press, 1991)

A. Brown, *Medicean and Savonarolan Florence: The Interplay of Politics, Humanism, and Religion* (Turnhout: Brepols, 2011)

M. P. Brown, *Understanding Illuminated Manuscripts: A Guide to Technical Terms* (London: J. Paul Getty Museum in association with the British Library, 1994)

M. P. Brown, *The Lindisfarne Gospels: Society, Spirituality and the Scribe* (London: British Library, 2003)

P. F. Brown, *Private Lives in Renaissance Venice: Art, Architecture, and the Family* (New Haven, London: Yale University Press, 2004)

W. De Clercq, J. Dumolyn and J. Haemers, '"Vivre Noblement": Material Culture and Elite Identity in Late Medieval Flanders', *Journal of Interdisciplinary History*, vol. 38, no. 1 (2007), pp. 1–31.

E. Currie, *Inside the Renaissance House* (London: V&A Publications, 2006)

C. De Hamel, *Scribes and Illuminators* (London: British Museum Press, 1992)

C. De Hamel, *A History of Illuminated Manuscripts* (2nd edn, revised, enl. and with new ill., London: Phaidon, 1994)

R. Dückers, *The Limbourg Brothers: Nijmegen Masters at the French Court, 1400–1416* (Ghent: Ludion, 2005)

R. Dückers and R. Priem (eds), *The Hours of Catherine of Cleves: Devotion, Demons and Daily Life in the Fifteenth Century* (Antwerp: Ludion; New York: Abrams, 2009)

G. Duby (ed.), *A History of Private Life*, vol. II: *Revelations of the Medieval World*, trans. A. Goldhammer (Cambridge, Mass.: Harvard University Press, 1987)

P. Eames, *Furniture in England, France and the Netherlands from the Twelfth to the Fifteenth Century* (London: Furniture History Society, 1977)

D. R. M. Gaimster (ed.), *Maiolica in the North: The Archaeology of Tin-Glazed Earthenware in North-West Europe c. 1500–1600. Proceedings of a colloquium hosted by the Department of Medieval and Later Antiquities on 6–7 March 1997* (London: British Museum Press, 1999)

R. A. Goldthwaite, *The Building of Renaissance Florence: An Economic and Social History* (Softshell books edn, Baltimore: Johns Hopkins University Press, 1990)

R. A. Goldthwaite, *The Economy of Renaissance Florence* (Baltimore: Johns Hopkins University Press, 2009)

The Grove Dictionary of Art Online

M. Hegarty, 'Laurentian Patronage in the Palazzo Vecchio: The Frescoes of the Sala dei Gigli', *The Art Bulletin*, vol. 78, no. 2 (1996), pp. 264–85

E. König , *Das liebentbrannte Herz: Der Wiener Codex und der Maler Barthélemy d'Eyck* (Graz: Akademische Druck- u. Verlagsanstalt, 1996)

E. König, *The Bedford Hours: The Making of a Medieval Masterpiece* (London: British Library, 2007)

T. Kren, *Illuminating the Renaissance: The Triumph of Flemish Manuscript Painting in Europe* (Los Angeles: J. Paul Getty Museum, 2003)

E. Mercer, *Furniture, 700–1700* (London: Weidenfeld & Nicolson, 1969)

L. Monnas, *Merchants, Princes and Painters: Silk Fabrics in Italian and Northern Paintings, 1300–1550* (New Haven, London: Yale University Press, 2008)

J. M. Musacchio, *Art, Marriage and Family in the Florentine Renaissance Palace* (New Haven, London: Yale University Press, 2008)

G. Nigro (ed.), *Francesco di Marco Datini: The Man, The Merchant* (Florence: Istituto Internazionale di Storia Economica F. Datini, 2010)

P. Nuttall, *From Flanders to Florence: The Impact of Netherlandish Painting, 1400–1500* (New Haven, London: Yale University Press, 2004)

I. Origo, *The Merchant of Prato: Francesco di Marco Datini* (London: Reprint Society, 1959)

C. Sciacca, *Building the Medieval World* (Los Angeles: J. Paul Getty Museum; London: British Library, 2010)

P. Spufford, *Power and Profit: The Merchant in Medieval Europe* (London: Thames & Hudson, 2002)

L. Syson and D. Thornton, *Objects of Virtue: Art in Renaissance Italy* (London: British Museum Press, 2001)

J. A. Testa, *The Beatty Rosarium: A Manuscript with Miniatures by Simon Bening* (Doornspijk, The Netherlands: Davaco Publishers, 1986)

D. Thornton, *The Scholar in His Study: Ownership and Experience in Renaissance Italy* (New Haven, London: Yale University Press, 1997)

P. Thornton, *The Italian Renaissance Interior 1400–1600* (London: Weidenfeld & Nicolson, 1991)

S. Thurley, *The Royal Palaces of Tudor England: Architecture and Court Life, 1460–1547* (New Haven, London: Yale University Press for the Paul Mellon Centre for Studies in British Art, 1993)

T. Wilson, *Italian Maiolica of the Renaissance* (Milan: Bocca, 1996)

Acknowledgements

This book was initially inspired by a series of fascinating and immensely enjoyable lectures given in the 1990s by Achim Hubel, professor and director of the Institut für Archäologie, Bauforschung und Denkmalpflege, Universität Bamberg, Germany. I would also like to express my gratitude to all the colleagues, friends and family who have helped and encouraged me in various ways during the process of writing this book.

My special thanks go to Bruce Barker-Benfield, Dirk Breiding, Michelle P. Brown, Patricia Buckingham, Silvia Castelli, Alessandro Cecchi, Matteo Ceriana, Ilaria Ciseri, Robert Davies, David Gaimster, Gillian Grant, Briony Hartley, Monika Jaglarz, Martin Kauffmann, Helen Langley, Giovanna Lazzi, Susy Marcon, Sally Nicholls, Richard Ovenden, Beatrice Paolozzi Majorca Strozzi, Sarah Patey, Zdzisław Pietrzyk, Katarzyna Plonka-Balus, Barbara Scholkmann, Magnolia Scudieri, Michela Sediari, Lara Speicher, Luke Syson, Sarah Thomas, David Thompson, Dora Thornton, Maria Grazia Vaccari and Adam Zamoyski.

INDEX